# Mary's Hours

# Mary's Hours

*Daily Prayers with the Mother of God*

Penelope Duckworth

Morehouse Publishing
NEW YORK · HARRISBURG · DENVER

Unless otherwise noted, the Scripture quotations contained herein are from the New Revised Standard Version Bible, copyright © 1989 by the Division of Christian Education of the National Council of Churches of Christ in the U.S.A. Used by permission. All rights reserved.

Morehouse Publishing, 4775 Linglestown Road, Harrisburg, PA 17112

Morehouse Publishing, 445 Fifth Avenue, New York, NY 10016

Morehouse Publishing is an imprint of Church Publishing Incorporated.

Cover art: Alejandra Vernon
Cover design by Laurie Klein Westhafer

Library of Congress Cataloging-in-Publication Data
Duckworth, Penelope, 1947-
Mary's hours : daily prayers with the Mother of God / Penelope Duckworth.
    p. cm.
Includes bibliographical references.
ISBN 978-0-8192-2342-5 (casebound)
1. Mary, Blessed Virgin, Saint--Prayers and devotions. 2. Anglican Communion–Prayers and devotions. 3. Episcopal Church--Prayers and devotions.  I. Title.
BT608.5.D83 2009
242'.74–dc22

2008046347

Printed in the United States of America


09 10 11 12 13 14        10 9 8 7 6 5 4 3 2 1

# TABLE OF CONTENTS

# ACKNOWLEDGMENTS

I would like to thank Michael Wilt, my friend and former editor at Cowley Publications, who first conceived the idea for this book. As a Roman Catholic, familiar with the traditional "Little Office of the Blessed Virgin Mary," he thought a contemporary prayer book which followed themes I had presented in my earlier book, "Mary: The Imagination of Her Heart" (Cowley, 2004) would be welcome. And I would like to thank Cynthia Shattuck, who has been my editor at Morehouse and has become my friend, for her wide knowledge and skillful editing which has both enhanced the book and brought it to fruition.

I am grateful to Alejandra Vernon whose art has now graced the cover of two of my books. I am indebted to the Sisters of the Community of Saint Francis in San Francisco for permission to quote from their Office Book. And I am thankful to those who have given me their work to use; Rosemarie Anderson, Alan Jones, Katherine Lehman, Barbara Newman, and Tony Stoneburner. I also wish to give special thanks to Elaine Kenseth-Abel and to the Sisters of the Discalced Carmelite Monastery in Pewaukee, WI, for permission to use copyrighted work, and I appreciate the help of all those who worked to assist me in securing permissions, especially Cindy Caruso, Sabina Lilly, Stephanie Munson, and Grainne Ross.

Finally, I would like to thank my own mother, who, at age 92, is a vibrant reminder of the fullness of life, and my husband, Dennis Gordon, and our daughter, Clare, for their love and support which has made this work both possible and richly meaningful.

# INTRODUCTION

"Redeem the time," the poet says, and this book is a means toward that end. It is a contemporary book of daily prayer that is a week-long cycle focused on devotion to God in Christ through the life of Mary. It is a book of liturgies (the word liturgy means "work of the people") that are called offices (which also means "work" and "offering"). But this office is an action and not a location; something we do rather than a place we go. So this book of offices is used to offer the work of a few minutes several times a day in the hope of redeeming the times of our lives. There are many kinds of prayer but all prayer is essentially being in relationship with God. This book offers both traditional and contemporary ways of being in the presence of God.

The roots of these daily offices are in that branch of Christianity known as the Anglican Communion and, more specifically, the Episcopal Church of the United States of America. Their older roots stretch back to the early Christian church and the daily liturgies of worship that evolved in the mornings and evenings of those fledgling communities; the roots then encompassed the monastic period in which daily worship was enlarged and enhanced. Some of those roots circled to enfold the growing devotion to Mary, "Theotokos," the Mother of God, and the devotional prayer books of the tenth century that first become known as the Little Office of the Blessed Virgin Mary. In time they became the basis of the favorite prayer book of the laity, often called a "Book of Hours," and many were richly illuminated with paintings, decorated capitals, and borders, including not only vivid colors but gold and other precious metals.

This far simpler "book of hours" begins on Sunday because it is understood in the church as the first day of the week. Each Sunday is traditionally a little Easter and celebrates the way in which the Resurrection, which took place at a certain point in time, now echoes through eternity. In the cycle of the church year and in our own souls, this festival of new life out of death and despair continues to circulate and reoccur. This book celebrates the Resurrection as perceived by Mary and the other women followers of Jesus who were both disciples as well as paradigms of Christian living.

Monday turns back to the beginning of the Christian story and focuses on the Joyful Mysteries, as they are called in the traditional rosary. We start with the Annunciation and Visitation, both of which reveal Mary's role as a prophet. Tuesday follows with the Birth, Presentation, and Flight into Egypt, looking at Mary as a matriarch and theologian. Wednesday continues focusing on Mary as a matriarch and theologian with the childhood incident of Jesus being lost in the temple, and introduces her role as intercessor with the miracle at the wedding in Cana. Thursday turns to Mary's discipleship and further celebrates her prophetic voice as the words of Jesus resonate with her influence. Other women who ministered to Jesus and to whom he ministered also figure in these offices.

On Friday, we turn to the Sorrowful Mysteries. Friday follows the tradition of the church down the ages by focusing on the

Passion and Crucifixion of Jesus and on Mary's role as disciple and intercessor. It also reminds us of her own suffering as she becomes Mother of Sorrows and we see her cosmic image as revealed in the Revelation of St. John the Divine. On Saturday, we continue with the theme of sorrow, but there is the beginning of hope. The cycle is completed as we turn again to the first of the Glorious Mysteries, which is Easter.

Morning and Evening Prayer have been part of Christian prayer life since the early church. Monastic life added other times for daily prayer and the 1979 Book of Common Prayer of the Episcopal Church added two of the older prayer offices—those of An Order of Service for Noonday, and Compline. In keeping with these additions, I have added Noon Prayer and Night Prayer to Morning and Evening Prayer. However, the Noon Prayer service has been varied to incorporate the Angelus, which is a traditional devotion in memory of the Incarnation, on Monday and Friday.

A wide variety of sources and translations have been used, in an effort to provide traditional forms as well as new, contemporary versions. Inclusive language has been preferred as well as fresh and prayerful translations. One traditional element of every office is a portion of the Psalms. I have sought to use psalms that are traditionally associated with Mary and that were favored in the medieval Books of Hours. In an effort to find psalms that use gender-free language for God, I am grateful for the work of Sister Cecilia of the Community of St. Francis in San Francisco, who has skillfully re-worded the psalms more inclusively than I ever thought possible.

Because the Lord's Prayer and the Magnificat are prayed every day, I have included in this book several translations. My hope is that they will give the reader a deepened appreciation of the meaning of the words of each. Other prayers as well as canticles have come from the rich variety of available liturgical sources, and the scripture chosen has come from a number of translations, ranging from William Tyndale's to Eugene Peterson's.

Although our piety is very different from the medieval mind, I have sought to include some canticles and prayers that resonate both with the sensibility of that era and with contemporary spirituality. I have also included a meditation with each office and have used a wide range of poetry and prose, including some of my own.

The compilation of this book of prayers with a focus on the life of Mary is intended to give those who use it a deeper appreciation of the life of the woman, traditionally recognized as first among the saints, who has been cherished as a soul friend by Christians since the beginning of the church. For that reason, several of the prayers are addressed to Mary. In prayers to Mary, it needs to be noted that we do not confuse her with God; rather, we pray to her as a companion who accompanies us on our soul's journey. For those new to this practice, it is helpful to know that prayer to Mary is an ancient practice; the first known prayer to Mary comes from the fourth century. The title of the book, *Mary's Hours*, urges us to set aside time to pray and reflect with Mary, and the subtitle emphasizes and urges us to remember her lifelong role as mother and nurturer.

This book is intended to be taken along and used throughout the day and evening. My hope is that it will become a trusted prayer resource that assists the user in moving into a deeper relationship with God while providing the adornment of prayer for the hours and days of life and thereby redeeming the time as it passes.

# ≈ SUNDAY ≈

## *Sunday Morning Prayer*

### Opening Sentence

Queen of heaven, rejoice, alleluia.
The Son whom you did merit to bear, alleluia,
has risen as He said, alleluia.
Pray God for us, alleluia.

### Canticle

Before I ventured forth, even while I was very young,
    I sought wisdom openly in my prayer.

In the forecourts of the temple I asked for her,
    and I will seek her to the end.

From the first blossom to the early fruit,
    she has been the delight of my heart.

My foot has kept firmly on the true path,
    diligently from my youth have I pursued her.

I inclined my ear a little and received her;
    I found for myself much wisdom and became adept in her.

To the one who gives me wisdom will I give glory,
  for I have resolved to live according to her way.
I directed my soul to her,
  and through purification have I found her.
From the beginning I gained courage from her,
  therefore I will not be forsaken.
In my inmost being have I been stirred to seek her,
  therefore have I gained a good possession.
As my reward the Almighty has given me the gift of language,
  and with it will I offer praise to God. *(Sirach 51:13–22)*

## Psalm 87

On the holy mountain stands the city you have founded;
  you love the gates of Zion
  more than all the dwellings of Jacob.

Glorious things are spoken of you,
  O city of our God.

I count Egypt and Babylon among those who know me;
  behold Philistia, Tyre, and Ethiopia:
  in Zion were they born.

Of Zion it shall be said, "Everyone was born in her,
  and the Most High shall sustain her."

God will record as the peoples are enrolled,
  "These also were born there."

The singers and dancers will say,
  "All my fresh springs are in you."

**Doxology**

Glory to God, Source of all being,
Eternal Word, and Holy Spirit;
as it was in the beginning, is now
and will be for ever. Amen.

**Scripture Reading**

As a vine, so brought I forth a savour of sweetness. And my flowers are the fruit of glory and riches. I am the mother of beautiful love and of fear, and of greatness and of holy hope. In me is all grace of life and truth. And in me is all hope of life and virtue. Come unto me all that desire me, and be filled with the fruits that spring from me. For my spirit is sweeter than honey or honeycomb. *(Sirach 24:17–20)*

**Meditation**

Christ is in the tomb as he was in his mother's womb, and just as that first silence was part of the rhythm that moved forward to the visible coming of life into the world, this silence in the tomb carries the music forward in three great beats to the hour when Life shall again come out of darkness and sweeten and sanctify the world.

Now as the music becomes audible again, it returns to its simplest form once more. It is lyrical again; at first only a man's breath stirring the flowers in a garden; and then a single word, the name of a friend spoken with indescribable love.

## The Lord's Prayer

Our Father in heaven,
    hallowed be your Name,
    your kingdom come,
    your will be done,
        on earth as in heaven.

Give us today our daily bread.

Forgive us our sins
    as we forgive those
        who sin against us.

Save us from the time of trial,
    and deliver us from evil.

For the kingdom, the power,
    and the glory are yours,
    now and for ever.  Amen.

## Prayer

Jesus our friend and guide, you demonstrated your love for us in the resurrection. Give us the responsive love of the three Marys who followed you to the cross, the grave, and the empty tomb. Give us grace to recognize and practice resurrection in this mortal life. Keep our faith warm and our hope green. We ask these things for your love's sake.  Amen.

**Blessing**

May the God who shakes heaven and earth,
whom death could not contain,
who lives to disturb and heal us,
bless you with power to go forth
and proclaim the gospel.
Amen.

## *Sunday Noon Prayer*

**Opening Sentence**

Angel at the tomb: "Whom do you seek?"
Women bearing spices: *"Jesus of Nazareth."*
Angel at the tomb: "He is not here, he has risen."
Women bearing spices: *"Alleluia, he has risen."*

**Canticle**

I pray to God who might
     save me as I hope.
Your help would be a blessing
     remembered by my successors;
that you would work your will
     through folk like us.
Your name is holy,
     because you aid the faithful.

Come in strength
>to foil the arrogant and deliver the humble.
Those who need you
>will be supplied.
Those who trust in themselves
>are deprived of your help.
Help me, oh God;
>your servant recalls your promises,
>made to my predecessors,
to Sarah and her descendants,
>who laugh at comic reversals!

## Psalm 98

Sing to our God a new song,
>for you have done marvelous things.

With your right hand and your holy arm
>have you won for yourself the victory.

You have made known your victory;
>your righteousness have you openly shown
>in the sight of the nations.

You remember your mercy and faithfulness
>to the house of Israel,
>and all the ends of the earth have seen the
>victory of our God.

Shout with joy to God, all you lands;
>lift up your voice, rejoice, and sing.

Sing to God with the harp,
>with the harp and the voice of song.

With trumpets and the sound of the horn
    shout with joy before our Sovereign God.

Let the sea make a noise and all that is in it,
    the lands and those who dwell therein.

Let the rivers clap their hands,
    and let the hills ring out with joy before our God,
    who comes to judge the earth.

In righteousness will you judge the world
    and the peoples with equity.


## Doxology

Glory be to God,
who made us;
who bears our pain;
and who loves us;
as it was in the beginning,
is now, and will be for ever. Amen.


## Scripture Reading

He said to me, "Mortal, can these bones live?" I answered, "O Lord GOD, you know." Then he said to me, "Prophesy to these bones, and say to them: O dry bones, hear the word of the LORD. Thus says the Lord GOD to these bones: I will cause breath to enter you, and you shall live. I will lay sinews on you, and will cause flesh to come upon you, and cover you with skin, and put breath in you, and you shall live; and you shall know that I am the LORD." *(Ezekiel 37:3–6)*

## Meditation

Whatever we do or gain in this world, let us consider it insignificant in comparison to the eternal wealth that is to come. We are on this earth as if in a second maternal womb. In that inner recess we did not have a life such as we have here, for we did not have there solid nourishment such as we enjoy now, nor were we able to be active as we are now, and we existed without the light of the sun and of any glimmer of light. Just as, then, when we were in that inner chamber, we did without many of the things of this world, so also in the present world we are impoverished in comparison with the kingdom of heaven. We have sampled the nourishment here; let us reach for the Divine! We have enjoyed the light of this world; let us long for the sun of righteousness! Let us regard the heavenly Jerusalem as our homeland.

## The Lord's Prayer

Seed and source,
>far in the distance and in our souls,
>you are holy and make us whole.

May we perceive your divine will
>that loved us into being

Help us to join your creative force
>and let it prosper here.

Give us what we need to survive,
>and release us from our transgressions,
>as we release others from theirs.

Keep us from away paths of destruction
>and from those who would ruin what you have made,
>for you are the matrix of life, love, and wisdom,
>now and forever. Amen.

**Prayer**

Father of love,
through your most Holy Spirit,
Mary the Jewish girl conceived your Son;
may his beauty, his humanity,
his all-transforming grace be born in us,
and may we never despise the strange and stirring gentleness
of your almighty power.
Amen.

**Blessing**

The peace of God,
the peace of God's people,
the peace of Mary mild, the loving one,
and of Christ, King of human hearts,
God's own peace. . .
be upon each thing our eyes take in,
be upon each thing our ears take in,
be upon our bodies which come from earth,
be upon our souls which come from heaven,
evermore and evermore,
Amen.

## *Sunday Evening Prayer*

### Opening Sentence

Hail, Queen of heaven;
hail, Mistress of the angels;
hail, root of Jesse;
hail, the gate through which the Light rose over the earth.

### Canticle

Alleluia! light
burst from your untouched
womb like a flower
on the farther side
of death. The world-tree
is blossoming. Two
realms become one.

### Psalm 103:1–18

Bless the Holy One, O my soul,
>and all that is within me, bless God's holy Name.

Bless the Holy One, O my soul,
>and forget not all God's benefits.

You forgive all our sins
>and heal all our infirmities.

You redeem our life from the grave
>and crown us with mercy and loving-kindness.

You satisfy us with good things,
>and our youth is renewed like an eagle's.

You execute righteousness
  and judgment for all who are oppressed.

You made your ways known to Moses
  and your works to the children of Israel.

You are full of compassion and mercy,
  slow to anger and of great kindness.

You will not always accuse us,
  nor will you keep your anger for ever.

You have not dealt with us according to our sins,
  nor rewarded us according to our wickedness.

For as the heavens are high above the earth,
  so is your mercy great upon those who fear you.

As far as the east is from the west,
  so far have you removed our sins from us.

As parents care for their children,
  so do you care for those who fear you.

For you know whereof we are made;
  you remember that we are but dust.

Our days are like the grass;
  we flourish like a flower of the field;

When the wind goes over it, it is gone,
  and its place shall know it no more.

But your merciful goodness endures for ever on those who fear you,
  and your righteousness on children's children;

On those who keep your covenant
  and remember your commandments and do them.

**Doxology**

Glory to God, our Creator,
to God's most Holy Word,
and to the Spirit, indwelling;
as it was in the beginning,
is now and will be for ever. Amen.

**Scripture Reading**

But Mary stood weeping outside the tomb. As she wept, she bent
over to look into the tomb; and she saw two angels in white, sitting
where the body of Jesus had been lying, one at the head and the
other at the feet. They said to her, "Woman, why are you weeping?" She said to them, "They have taken away my Lord, and I do
not know where they have laid him." When she had said this, she
turned around and saw Jesus standing there, but she did not know
that it was Jesus. Jesus said to her, "Woman, why are you weeping? Whom are you looking for?" Supposing him to be the gar-
dener, she said to him, "Sir, if you have carried him away, tell me
where you have laid him, and I will take him away." Jesus said to
her, "Mary!" She turned and said to him in Hebrew, "Rabbouni!"
(which means Teacher). Jesus said to her, "Do not hold on to me,
because I have not yet ascended to the Father. But go to my brothers and say to them, 'I am ascending to my Father and your Father,
to my God and your God.'" Mary Magdalene went and announced
to the disciples, "I have seen the Lord"; and she told them that he
had said these things to her. *(John 20:11–18)*

**Meditation**

Life is yours forever, Mary,
for your light is come once more
and the strength of death is broken;
now your songs of joy outpour.
Ended now the night of sorrow,
Love has brought the blessed morrow.
Let your alleluias rise!

**The Lord's Prayer**

Our Father in heaven,
Reveal who you are.
Set the world right;
Do what's best—
          as above, so below.
Keep us alive with three square meals.
Keep us forgiven with you and forgiving others.
Keep us safe from ourselves and the Devil.

**Prayer**

God,
you are our beginning and you will be our end;
we are made in your image and likeness.
We praise and thank you for this day.
This is the day on which you created light
and saw that it was good.
This is the day in whose early morning light
we discovered the tomb was empty,
and encountered Christ, the world's true light.

For us your acts are gracious
and your love endures forever.

O divine Master,
grant that we may not so much seek to be consoled,
as to console;
to be understood, as to understand;
to be loved, as to love.
For it is in giving that we receive;
it is in pardoning that we are pardoned;
it is in dying that we are born to eternal life.

Jesus our inspiration,
you come in the evening as our doors are shut,
and bring peace.
Grant us sleep tonight,
and courage tomorrow to go wherever you lead.
Amen.

## Blessing

May the joy of the three Marys be with us:
the joy of Mary Magdalene, who beheld her friend raised and alive;
the joy of Mary, the contemplative sister, who beheld her
        answered prayer;
and the joy of the Blessed Mother, who beheld her resurrected child.
May friendship with God, the conversation of prayer,
        and Christ born within us
be our soul's path and joy.  Amen.

## *Sunday Night Prayer*

**Opening Sentence**

Birth-giver of God, you are graced! Alleluia!
For Christ the fruit of your womb has been raised!
  Alleluia!
He is risen and we with him! Alleluia!
Your blest consent has done this! Alleluia!

**Canticle**

The child you bore has risen now
and stayed the pow'r of death and sin.
See him stand—
with holes and heaven in his hand.

**Psalm 131**

O God, I am not proud;
  I have no haughty looks.

I do not occupy myself with great matters,
  or with things that are too hard for me.

But I still my soul and make it quiet,
like a child upon its mother's breast;
  my soul is quieted within me.

O Israel, wait upon our God,
  from this time forth for evermore.

**Doxology**

Glory be to the Father, and to the Son, and to the Holy Spirit: as it was in the beginning, is now, and will be for ever. Amen.

**Scripture Reading**

At that time Jesus said, "I thank you, Father, Lord of heaven and earth, because you have hidden these things from the wise and the intelligent and have revealed them to infants; yes, Father, for such was your gracious will. All things have been handed over to me by my Father; and no one knows the Son except the Father, and no one knows the Father except the Son and anyone to whom the Son chooses to reveal him.

"Come to me, all you that are weary and are carrying heavy burdens, and I will give you rest. Take my yoke upon you, and learn from me; for I am gentle and humble in heart, and you will find rest for your souls. For my yoke is easy, and my burden is light." *(Matthew 11:25–30)*

**Meditation**

What they then felt—is it not sweet
above all secrets
and yet an earthly, human thing,
that he, a little pale still from the tomb,
went toward her, disburdened,
wholly resurrected?
Oh, first to her. How they were then
being healed unspeakably.
Yes, they were healing. That was it.

They did not need to touch each other firmly.
Barely an instant
he laid his soon-to-be-eternal hand
upon the womanly shoulder.
And they began,
silently as trees in spring,
infinitely together,
this season of their uttermost communion.

**The Lord's Prayer**

Our Father, who art in heaven,
 hallowed be thy Name,
 thy kingdom come,
 thy will be done,
  on earth as it is in heaven.

Give us this day our daily bread.

And forgive us our trespasses,
 as we forgive those
  who trespass against us.

And lead us not into temptation,
 but deliver us from evil.

For thine is the kingdom,
 and the power, and the glory,
 for ever and ever.  Amen.

## Prayer

Loving God, we give you thanks that each Sunday reminds us of the resurrection of Jesus. Give us grace to practice resurrection in our daily life, and with it to find the joy and wonder of the holy women and men who met the Resurrected Lord and learned that sacrificing love overcomes death. We ask this in the name of Christ, who with you and the Holy Spirit lives and reigns, now and forever. Amen.

## Blessing

We turn to you for protection,
holy Mother of God.
Listen to our prayers
and help us in our needs.
Save us from every danger,
glorious and blessed Virgin.
Amen.

# ☙ MONDAY ❧

## *Monday Morning Prayer*

### Opening Sentence

Look, the young woman is with child and shall bear a son, and shall name him Immanuel. *(Isaiah 7:14)*

### Canticle

My heart exults in the Lord:
    my strength is exalted in my God.

There is none holy like the Lord,
    there is none beside you, no rock like our God.

For you O Lord are a God of knowledge:
    and by you our actions are weighed.

The bows of the mighty are broken:
    but the feeble gird on strength.

You Lord make poor and make rich:
    you bring low and you also exalt.

You raise up the poor from the dust:
    you lift the needy from the ashheap.

You make them sit with princes:
>    and inherit a seat of honour.

For yours O Lord are the pillars of the earth:
>    and on them you have set the world.
>    *(I Samuel 2:1–4, 7–8)*


## Psalm 114

Hallellujah!
When Israel came out of Egypt,
>    the house of Jacob from a people of strange speech,

Judah became God's sanctuary
>    and Israel God's dominion.

The sea beheld it and fled;
>    Jordan turned and went back.

The mountains skipped like rams,
>    and the little hills like young sheep.

What ailed you, O sea, that you fled?
>    O Jordan, that you turned back?

You mountains, that you skipped like rams?
>    you little hills like young sheep?

Tremble, O earth, at the presence of God,
>    at the presence of the God of Jacob,

Who turned the hard rock into a pool of water
>    and flint-stone into a flowing spring.

**Doxology**

Glory to God, Source of all being,
Eternal Word, and Holy Spirit;
as it was in the beginning, is now
and will be for ever.  Amen.

**Scripture Reading**

In the sixth month the angel Gabriel was sent by God to a town
in Galilee called Nazareth, to a virgin engaged to a man whose
name was Joseph, of the house of David. The virgin's name was
Mary. And he came to her and said, "Greetings, favored one! The
Lord is with you." But she was much perplexed by his words and
pondered what sort of greeting this might be. The angel said to
her, "Do not be afraid, Mary, for you have found favor with God.
And now, you will conceive in your womb and bear a son, and you
will name him Jesus. He will be great, and will be called the Son
of the Most High, and the Lord God will give to him the throne of
his ancestor David. He will reign over the house of Jacob forever,
and of his kingdom there will be no end." Mary said to the angel,
"How can this be, since I am a virgin?" The angel said to her, "The
Holy Spirit will come upon you, and the power of the Most High
will overshadow you; therefore the child to be born will be holy;
he will be called Son of God. And now, your relative Elizabeth in
her old age has also conceived a son; and this is the sixth month
for her who was said to be barren.  For nothing will be impossible
with God." Then Mary said, "Here am I, the servant of the Lord;
let it be with me according to your word." Then the angel departed
from her. *(Luke 1:26–38)*

## Meditation

*Gabriel remembers:*

It was early spring and I emerged
      in a dawn orchard where sky
and blossom shone the color
      of the cheek I touched and she
turned surprised. Then I told her
      and when she questioned me, my cheek
burned—not with indignation but
      the possibility of partnership.
She walked with me toward apple trees,
      the sun was bold through new leaves and
I learned the reason behind the message
      because I, too, now loved the world.

## The Lord's Prayer

Eternal Spirit,
Pain-bearer, Love-maker, Life-giver,
Source of all that is and that shall be,
Father and Mother of us all,
Loving God, in whom is heaven:

The hallowing of your name echo through the universe!
The way of your justice be followed by the peoples of the world!
Your heavenly will be done by all created beings!
Your commonwealth of peace and freedom sustain our hope and
come on earth.

With the bread we need for today, feed us.
In the hurts we absorb from one another, forgive us.
In times of temptation and test, strengthen us.
From trials too great to endure, spare us.
From the grip of all that is evil, free us.
For you reign in the glory of the power that is love, now and
for ever.  Amen.


**Prayer**

Holy One, whose angels are still working among us, and who sends
us messages through scripture, nature, prayer, dreams, friends,
and enemies: help us pay attention to your promptings so that our
response to you is lives lived, as Mary's was, according to your
word. We ask this in the name of Jesus, our Savior, who lives and
reigns with you and the Holy Spirit, now and forever.  Amen.


**Blessing**

May the Holy Spirit,
by whose overshadowing Mary become the Godbearer,
give you grace to carry the good news of Christ.  Amen.

## *Monday Noon Prayer*

### Opening Sentence

Scripture says that God's greatest gift is that we are his children and that he begets his Son in us. The supreme purpose of God is birth. He will not be content until his Son is born in us.

### Psalm 126

When God restored the fortunes of Zion,
>> then were we like those who dream.

Then was our mouth filled with laughter,
>> and our tongue with shouts of joy.

Then they said among the nations,
>> "God has done great things for them."

God has done great things for us,
>> and we are glad indeed.

Restore our fortunes, O God,
>> like the watercourses of the Negev.

Those who sowed with tears
>> will reap with songs of joy.

Those who go out weeping, carrying the seed,
>> will come again with joy, shouldering their sheaves.

**Doxology**

Glory be to God,
who made us;
who bears our pain;
and who loves us;
as it was in the beginning,
is now, and will be for ever.  Amen.

**Scripture Reading**

And Mary arose in those days, and went into the mountains with haste, into a city of Jewry and entered into the house of Zachary, and saluted Elizabeth. And it fortuned, as Elizabeth heard the salutation of Mary, the babe sprang in her belly. And Elizabeth was filled with the holy ghost, and cried with a loud voice, and said: Blessed art thou among women, and blessed is the fruit of thy womb. And whence happeneth this to me, that the mother of my Lord should come to me? For lo, as soon as the voice of thy salutation sounded in mine ears, the babe sprang in my belly for joy. And blessed art thou that believedst: for those things shall be performed which were told thee from the Lord. *(Luke 1:39–45 Tyndale)*

**Meditation**

The second bead: scene of the lovely journey
of Lady Mary, on whom artists confer
a blue silk gown, a day pouring out Springtime,
and birds singing and flowers bowing to her.

Rather, I see a girl upon a donkey
and her, too held by what was said, to mind
how the sky was or if the grass was growing.
I doubt the flowers; I doubt the road was kind.

"Love hurried forth to serve," I read, approving.
But also see, with thoughts blown past her youth,
a girl riding upon a jolting donkey
and riding further and further into the truth.

## The Lord's Prayer

Our Father, who art in heaven,
     hallowed be thy Name,
     thy kingdom come
     thy will be done,
          on earth as it is in heaven.

Give us this day our daily bread.

And forgive us our trespasses,
     as we forgive those
          who trespass against us.

And lead us not into temptation,
     but deliver us from evil.

For thine is the kingdom,
     and the power, and the glory,
     for ever and ever.  Amen.

**The Angelus**

*The Angel of the Lord announced to Mary, and she conceived by the Holy Spirit.*

Hail Mary, full of grace, the Lord is with you. Blessed are you among women, and blessed is the fruit of your womb, Jesus.

Holy Mary, Mother of God, pray for us sinners, now and at the hour of our death. Amen.

*I am the handmaid of the Lord; let it be to me according to your word.*

Hail Mary, full of grace, the Lord is with you. Blessed are you among women, and blessed is the fruit of your womb, Jesus.

Holy Mary, Mother of God, pray for us sinners, now and at the hour of our death. Amen.

*And the Word was made Flesh and lived among us.*

Hail Mary, full of grace, the Lord is with you. Blessed are you among women, and blessed is the fruit of your womb, Jesus.

Holy Mary, Mother of God, pray for us sinners, now and at the hour of our death. Amen.

*Pray for us, O holy Mother of God,*
*that we may be made worthy of the promises of Christ.*

## Prayer

Pour your grace into our hearts, O Lord, that we who have known the incarnation of your Son Jesus Christ, announced by an angel to the Virgin Mary, may by his cross and passion be brought to the glory of his resurrection; who lives and reigns with you, in the unity of the Holy Spirit, one God, now and for ever. Amen.

## Blessing

May the blessing of the God of Abraham and Sarah, and of Jesus Christ born of our sister Mary, and of the Holy Spirit, who broods over the world as a mother over her children, be upon us and remain with us always. Amen.

## *Monday Evening Prayer*

### Opening Sentence

If you meet the Virgin
coming down the road,
ask her into your house.
She bears the word of God.

## Canticle

My soul proclaims the greatness of the Lord,
my spirit rejoices in God my Savior;
>    for you, Lord, have looked with favor on your lowly servant.

From this day all generations will call me blessed:
>    you, the Almighty, have done great things for me,
>    and holy is your name.

You have mercy on those who fear you
>    from generation to generation.

You have shown strength with your arm
>    and scattered the proud in their conceit,

Casting down the mighty from their thrones
>    and lifting up the lowly.

You have filled the hungry with good things
>    and sent the rich away empty.

You have come to the aid of your servant Israel,
>    to remember the promise of mercy,
The promise made to our forebears,
>    to Abraham and his children for ever.


## Psalm 84:1–9

How dear to me is your dwelling, O God of hosts!
>    My soul has a desire and longing for the courts
>        of the Most High;
>    my heart and my flesh rejoice in the living God.

The sparrow has found her a house
>and the swallow a nest where she may lay her young;
>by the side of your altars, O God of hosts,
>my Sovereign and my God.

Happy are they who dwell in your house!
>they will always be praising you.

Happy are the people whose strength is in you!
>whose hearts are set on the pilgrims' way.

Those who go through the desolate valley will find
>>it a place of springs,
>for the early rains have covered it with pools of water.

They will climb from height to height,
>and the God of gods will be revealed in Zion.

God of hosts, hear my prayer;
>hearken, O God of Jacob.

Behold our defender, O God;
>and look upon the face of your Anointed.

For one day in your courts is better than
>>a thousand in my own room,
>and to stand at the threshold of the house of my God
>than to dwell in the tents of the wicked.

**Doxology**

Glory be to the Father, and to the Son, and to the Holy Spirit:
as it was in the beginning, is now, and will be for ever.  Amen.

## Scripture Reading

But you, O Bethlehem of Ephrathah,
     who are one of the little clans of Judah,
from you shall come forth for me
     one who is to rule in Israel,
whose origin is from of old,
     from ancient days.
Therefore he shall give them up until the time
     when she who is in labor has brought forth;
then the rest of his kindred shall return
     to the people of Israel.
And he shall stand and feed his flock
          in the strength of the LORD,
     in the majesty of the name of the LORD his God.
And they shall live secure, for now he shall be great
     to the ends of the earth;
and he shall be the one of peace. *(Micah 5:2–5)*

## Meditation

The angel summoned Mary, betrothed to Joseph, from the rather safe place of conventional wisdom to a realm where few of the old rules would make much sense. She entered that unknown called "virgin territory." She was on her own there. No one else could judge for her the validity of her experience.

She can measure her reality against Scripture, the teachings of her tradition, her reason and intellect, and the counsel of wise friends. But finally it is up to her. The redemption of the creation is resting on the consent—the choice of this mortal woman to believe fearlessly that what she is experiencing is true. And to claim and live out that truth by conceiving the fruit of salvation.

To be virgin means to be one, whole in oneself, not perforated by the concerns of the conventional norms and authority, or the powers and principalities.

**The Lord's Prayer**

Our Father in heaven,
> hallowed be your Name,
> your kingdom come,
> your will be done,
>> on earth as in heaven.

Give us today our daily bread.

Forgive us our sins
> as we forgive those
>> who sin against us.

Save us from the time of trial,
> and deliver us from evil.

For the kingdom, the power,
> and the glory are yours,
> now and for ever.  Amen.

**Prayer**

For whatever in us hears thee coming among us, stirring the season, sending the rains, moving the buds, running the robins—we rejoice and will rejoice, great Lord. For whatever in us sees thee going before us, breaking a new path, clearing a troubled mind, awaking a sleeping town, turning our purpose—we rejoice and will rejoice, good Lord. For whatever in us touches thee standing among us, shaping our prayers, healing our sick, breaking our evil, giving us vision—we rejoice and will rejoice, dear Lord. Praise is in us. Magnify that praise. Amen.

**Blessing**

If Mary protects me
her divine Son
will receive me
into the company of the saints
who walk with him in paradise.

Like a lost sheep
whose shepherd is searching for it,
seek me, Mother of mercy.
Bring me safely home.

## *Monday Night Prayer*

### Opening Sentence

I sing a maid of tender years
To whom an angel came,
And knelt, as to a mighty queen,
And bowed bright wings of flame.

### Canticle

God that madest earth and heaven,
  Darkness and light;
Who the day for toil hast given,
  For rest the night;
May thine angel guards defend us,
Slumber sweet thy mercy send us,
Holy dreams and hopes attend us,
  This livelong night.

Guard us waking, guard us sleeping,
  And, when we die,
May we in thy mighty keeping
  All peaceful lie:
When the last dread call shall wake us,
Do not thou our God forsake us,
But to reign in glory take us
  With thee on high.

## Psalm 71:1–6

In you, O God, have I taken refuge;
    let me never be ashamed.

In your righteousness, deliver me and set me free;
    incline your ear to me and save me.

Be my strong rock, a castle to keep me safe;
    you are my crag and my stronghold.

Deliver me, my God, from the hand of the wicked,
    from the clutches of the evildoer and the oppressor.

For you are my hope, O God,
    my confidence since I was young.

I have been sustained by you ever since I was born;
from my mother's womb you have been my strength;
    my praise shall be always of you.

## Doxology

Glory to God, our Creator,
to God's most Holy Word,
and to the Spirit, indwelling;
as it was in the beginning,
is now and will be for ever. Amen.

## Scripture Reading

Then the word of the LORD came unto me, saying, Before I formed thee in the belly I knew thee; and before thou camest forth out of the womb I sanctified thee, and I ordained thee a prophet unto the nations. Then said I, Ah, Lord GOD! behold, I cannot speak: for I am a child.

But the LORD said unto me, Say not, I am a child: for thou shalt go to all that I shall send thee, and whatsoever I command thee thou shalt speak. Be not afraid of their faces: for I am with thee to deliver thee, saith the LORD. Then the LORD put forth his hand, and touched my mouth. And the LORD said unto me, Behold, I have put my words in thy mouth. *(Jeremiah 1:4–9 KJV)*

## Meditation

If Mary had not heard, had heard
but had not listened,
had understood but not stood
still, had not consented,
had been scared
and had scurried from the garden
where he glistened
into the dark house or the dark wood,
worried because the Word he hinted
stirred
uneasily within the ear; if she had erred
and had permitted heart to harden
when, like frost enameled ground, air glinted,
the Word would have been only sound.

## The Lord's Prayer

Our heavenly Father, hallowed is your name.
Your Kingdom is come. Your will is done,
      as in heaven so also on earth.
Give us the bread for our daily need.
And leave us serene,
      just as we also allowed others serenity.
And do not pass us through trial,
      except separate us from the evil one.
For yours is the Kingdom,
      the Power and the Glory
to the end of the universe, of all the universes.  Amen!

## Prayer

O unknown God,
whose presence is announced
not among the impressive
but in obscurity;
come, overshadow us now,
and speak to our hidden places;
that, entering your darkness with joy,
we may choose to cooperate with you,
through Jesus Christ.  Amen.

## Blessing

The wind is like Gabriel and you are like Mary,
      Jesus the face of flower, born from these two.
The dancing of you two is the key to eternity.
      May God bless this dance.

# TUESDAY

## *Tuesday Morning Prayer*

**Opening Sentence**

Come abide within us; let my soul like Mary,
be thine earthly sanctuary.

**Canticle**

In the beginning was the Word:
>and the Word was with God;

and the Word was God:
>he was in the beginning with God.

All things were made through him:
>and without him
>was not anything made that was made.

In him was life:
>and the life was the light of the human race.

The light shines in the darkness:
>and the darkness has never overcome it.

He was in the world,
>and the world was made through him:
>yet the world knew him not.

He came to his own home:
>and his own people would not receive him.

But to all who received him,
>who believed on his name:
>he has given power to become children of God.

And the Word became flesh:
>and dwelt among us, full of grace and truth.
>>*(John 1:1–5, 10–14)*

## Psalm 119:89–96

O God, your word is everlasting;
>it stands firm in the heavens.

Your faithfulness remains from one generation to another;
>you established the earth, and it abides.

By your decree these continue to this day,
>for all things are your servants.

If my delight had not been in your law,
>I should have perished in my affliction.

I will never forget your commandments,
>because by them you give me life.

I am yours; oh, that you would save me!
>for I study your commandments.

Though the wicked lie in wait for me to destroy me,
>I will apply my mind to your decrees.

I see that all things come to an end,
>but your commandment has no bounds.

**Doxology**

Glory be to the Father, and to the Son, and to the Holy Spirit: as it was in the beginning, is now, and will be for ever. Amen.

**Scripture Reading**

In those days a decree went out from Emperor Augustus that all the world should be registered. This was the first registration and was taken while Quirinius was governor of Syria. All went to their own towns to be registered. Joseph also went from the town of Nazareth in Galilee to Judea, to the city of David called Bethlehem, because he was descended from the house and family of David. He went to be registered with Mary, to whom he was engaged and who was expecting a child. While they were there, the time came for her to deliver her child. And she gave birth to her firstborn son and wrapped him in bands of cloth, and laid him in a manger, because there was no place for them in the inn.

In that region there were shepherds living in the fields, keeping watch over their flock by night. Then an angel of the Lord stood before them, and the glory of the Lord shone around them, and they were terrified. *(Luke 2:1–9)*

**Meditation**

The frightened shepherds become God's messengers. They organize, make haste, find others, and speak with them. Do we not all want to become shepherds and catch sight of the angel? I think so. Without the perspective of the poor, we see nothing, not even an angel. When we approach the poor, our values and goals change. The child appears in many other children. Mary also seeks sanctuary among us. Because the angels sing, the shepherds rise, leave their fears behind, and set out for Bethlehem, wherever it is situated these days.

## The Lord's Prayer

Holy One,
> we honor your name.

Let the world know your justice
> here as everywhere.

Give us the food we need
> both for the body and the soul.

Forgive us the wrongs we do
> as we forgive the wrongs of others.

Keep us safe from the evil
> at large or of our own making.

We trust you for you made us and
> we are yours, now and always.  Amen.

## Prayer

God our beloved,
born of a woman's body:
you came that we might look upon you,
and handle you with our own hands.
May we so cherish one another in our bodies
that we may also be touched by you;
through the Word made flesh, Jesus Christ.
Amen.

**Blessing**

May God write a message upon your heart,
bless and direct you,
then send you out,
living letters of the Word.
Amen.

## Tuesday Noon Prayer

**Opening Sentence**

She will bear a son, and you are to name him Jesus, for he will
save his people from their sins. *(Matthew 1:21)*

**Canticle**

The Virgin gives birth to the Inexpressible,
and the earth offers a cave to the Unapproachable;
angels and shepherds together give glory,
and the Magi are guided by a star,
when for our sakes was born, as a new babe,
the one who from eternity is God.

**Psalm 30:1–6**

I will exalt you, O God,
because you have lifted me up
and have not let my enemies triumph over me.

O my God, I cried out to you,
>and you restored me to health.

You brought me up, O God, from the dead;
>you restored my life as I was going down to the grave.

Sing to the Most High, you who serve our God;
>give thanks for the remembrance of God's holiness.

For the wrath of God endures but the twinkling of an eye,
>God's favor for a lifetime.

Weeping may spend the night,
>but joy comes in the morning.

### Doxology

Glory to God, our Creator,
to God's most Holy Word,
and to the Spirit, indwelling;
as it was in the beginning,
is now and will be for ever.

### Scripture Reading

But the angel said to them, "Do not be afraid; for see—I am bringing you good news of great joy for all the people: to you is born this day in the city of David a Savior, who is the Messiah, the Lord. This will be a sign for you: you will find a child wrapped in bands of cloth and lying in a manger." . . .

When the angels had left them and gone into heaven, the shepherds said to one another, "Let us go now to Bethlehem and see this thing that has taken place, which the Lord has made known to us." So they went with haste and found Mary and

Joseph, and the child lying in the manger. When they saw this, they made known what had been told them about this child; and all who heard it were amazed at what the shepherds told them. But Mary treasured all these words and pondered them in her heart. *(Luke 2:10–12, 15–19)*

## Meditation

*Joseph speaks:*
His birth wasn't anything special.
Mary anxious of course—far from home.
I was really thrown by that funny dream
(before the trek to Bethlehem),
that story-book angel telling me not to worry,
announcing that Mary's belly was swollen with—
what did he say?—
Immanuel?

Accommodations weren't of the best,
but the baby came all the same,
greeted by sweaty animals
and a few derelict shepherds.

Still the baby's eyes are clear,
his grip is strong.
I have great hopes for our Immanuel.
You never know.
God knows, with the roads unsafe and
the Romans not about to leave,
we could do with
a prince of peace.

## The Lord's Prayer

Eternal Spirit,
Pain-bearer, Love-maker, Life-giver,
Source of all that is and that shall be,
Father and Mother of us all,
Loving God, in whom is heaven:

The hallowing of your name echo through the universe!
The way of your justice be followed by the peoples of the world!
Your heavenly will be done by all created beings!
Your commonwealth of peace and freedom sustain our hope and
come on earth.

With the bread we need for today, feed us.
In the hurts we absorb from one another, forgive us.
In times of temptation and test, strengthen us.
From trials too great to endure, spare us.
From the grip of all that is evil, free us.
For you reign in the glory of the power that is love, now and
for ever. Amen.


## Prayer

Loving God, who places us in families that we may experience
and grow in love, give us grace in the midst of our days to ponder
your loving-kindness and to reflect on the love that has come to
us through others. Help us, like Mary, to treasure your presence in
the unique situations of our lives, and give us grace to show your
love to those who have not known it. We ask this in the name of
him who came among us helpless and first learned love through
his mother. Amen.

**Blessing**

The joy of God shine from your face
and joy to all who see you;
the shield of God surround your head,
and angels ever guard you.
May every season be good for you
and the Son of Mary give peace to you.
Amen.

## *Tuesday Evening Prayer*

**Opening Sentence**

The word of God is living and active, sharper than any two-edged sword, piercing until it divides soul from spirit, joints from marrow; it is able to judge the thoughts and intentions of the heart. *(Hebrews 4:12)*

**Canticle**

Lord, now lettest thou thy servant depart in peace,
    according to thy word;

For mine eyes have seen thy salvation,
    which thou hast prepared before the face of all people,

To be a light to lighten the Gentiles,
    and to be the glory of thy people Israel.  Amen.

### Psalm 119:105–112

Your word is a lantern to my feet
      and a light upon my path.

I have sworn and am determined
      to keep your righteous judgments.

I am deeply troubled;
      preserve my life according to your word.

Accept the willing tribute of my lips,
      and teach me your judgments.

My life is always in my hand,
      yet I do not forget your law.

The wicked have set a trap for me,
      but I have not strayed from your commandments.

Your decrees are my inheritance for ever;
      truly, they are the joy of my heart.

I have applied my heart to fulfill your statutes
      for ever and to the end.

### Doxology

Glory to God, Source of all being,
Eternal Word, and Holy Spirit;
as it was in the beginning, is now
and will be for ever.  Amen.

## Scripture Reading

And Simeon blessed them, and said unto Mary his mother: behold, this child shall be the fall and resurrection of many in Israel, and a sign which shall be spoken against. And moreover the sword shall pierce thy soul, that the thoughts of many hearts may be opened.

And there was a prophetess, one Anna, the daughter of Phanuel of the tribe of Aser: which was of a great age, and had lived with an husband seven years from her virginity. And she had been a widow about four score and four years, which went never out of the temple, but served God with fasting and prayer night and day. And the same came forth that same hour, and praised the Lord, and spake of him to all that looked for redemption in Jerusalem. *(Luke 2:34-38 Tyndale)*

## Meditation

I stand beside the temple pillar.
I watch and wait, testing this wonder.
Is the time at last arriving?
Has Yahweh entered a house of clay?
Only when Simeon whispered the sword,
I felt unpinned from mortal pain.
A grief was there but six-winged solace
sang the same tone as the sunlight,
incongruous with the young wife
holding the recently bartered pigeons,
her husband's eyes fresh from dreaming,
the gurgling child in ancient arms.

I hum in the shadows, just simple words come,
I trust the plain words, make this song:

*A birthday always has a deathday,*
*a sword starts coming down the years,*
*a birthday always has a deathday,*
*reminding us with blood and tears.*
*A child is here—a sword is coming.*
*A child is here—to stop its sting,*
*a child whose deathday has a birthday,*
*a child reversing everything.*


## The Lord's Prayer

Our Father in heaven,
      hallowed be your Name,
      your kingdom come,
      your will be done,
         on earth as in heaven.

Give us today our daily bread.

Forgive us our sins
      as we forgive those
         who sin against us.

Save us from the time of trial,
      and deliver us from evil.

For the kingdom, the power,
      and the glory are yours,
      now and for ever.  Amen.

**Prayer**

O Majesty, behold in pity what we are. Turn aside from thy mountains and thy stars and have mercy upon us. For we dwell in sin. We are proud in the imagination of our hearts. We make wars. We send the hungry empty away. We are lazy before thy truth, and casual and crude in the holy places. We have sought our own safety, denied justice, overlooked falsehood, applauded greed. We have sown the wind and reaped the whirlwind. Come to us, good Lord. Defend us from ourselves; and by thy enormous forgiveness, restore in us a right mind, a faithful heart, and a rejoicing soul; through Jesus Christ our Lord. Amen.

**Blessing**

May God, who sent us the light of the world
and who has given us the light of this day,
grant that we may come to know the lightness of being
which allowed Mary to say, "Yes." Amen.

## *Tuesday Night Prayer*

**Opening Sentence**

May you cling to His most sweet Mother who gave birth to a Son whom the heavens could not contain. And yet she carried Him in the little enclosure of her holy womb and held Him on her virginal lap.

## Canticle

Tell out, my soul, the greatness of the Lord!
Unnumbered blessings give my spirit voice;
tender to me the promise of his word;
in God my Savior shall my heart rejoice.

Tell out, my soul, the greatness of his Name!
Make known his might, the deeds his arm has done;
his mercy sure, from age to age the same;
his holy Name—the Lord, the Mighty One.

Tell out, my soul, the greatness of his might!
Powers and dominions lay their glory by.
Proud hearts and stubborn wills are put to flight,
the hungry fed, the humble lifted high.

Tell out, my soul, the glories of his word!
Firm is his promise, and his mercy sure.
Tell out, my soul, the greatness of the Lord
to children's children and for evermore!


## Psalm 121

I lift up my eyes to the hills;
>from where is my help to come?

My help comes from our God,
the maker of heaven and earth.

God will not let your foot be moved;
the one who watches over you will not fall asleep.

Behold, the one who keeps watch over Israel
shall neither slumber nor sleep;

The Holy One watches over you;
>God is your shade at your right hand,

So that the sun shall not strike you by day,
>nor the moon by night.

God will preserve you from all evil;
>the Most High will keep you safe.

God will watch over your going out and your coming in,
>from this time forth for evermore.

**Doxology**

Glory be to God,
who made us;
who bears our pain;
and who loves us;
as it was in the beginning,
is now, and will be for ever.  Amen.

**Scripture Reading**

Now after [the Magi] had left, an angel of the Lord appeared to Joseph in a dream and said, "Get up, take the child and his mother, and flee to Egypt, and remain there until I tell you; for Herod is about to search for the child, to destroy him." Then Joseph got up, took the child and his mother by night, and went to Egypt, and remained there until the death of Herod. This was to fulfill what had been spoken by the Lord through the prophet, "Out of Egypt I have called my son." *(Matthew 2:13–15)*

## Meditation

How fresh, O Lord, how sweet and clean
Are thy returns! Ev'n as the flowers in spring;
    To which, besides their own demean,
The late past tributes of pleasure bring.
        Grief melts away
        Like snow in May,
     As if there were no such cold thing.

    Who would have thought my shrivel'd heart
Could have recover'd greenesse? It was gone
    Quite underground; as flowers depart
To see their mother-root, when they have blown;
        Where they together
        All the hard weather,
     Dead to the world, keep house unknown.

## The Lord's Prayer

Our Father, who art in heaven,
    hallowed be thy Name,
    thy kingdom come
    thy will be done,
        on earth as it is in heaven.

Give us this day our daily bread.

And forgive us our trespasses,
    as we forgive those
        who trespass against us.

And lead us not into temptation,
    but deliver us from evil.

For thine is the kingdom,
and the power, and the glory,
    for ever and ever.  Amen.

## Prayer

Loving God, who holds this beautiful, endangered world as a mother holds her child: give us grace so to live that others may enjoy the riches of creation, and experience the justice, mercy and kindness you require of us, through our Savior Jesus Christ, who with you and the Holy Spirit lives and loves, one God, now and forever.  Amen.

## Blessing

May Jesus, our infant redeemer, give us the joy of the shepherds as they ran to the stable, the awe of the magi as they knelt before the child, and the faith of the holy family as they found themselves at the center of God's saving love. Amen.

# ≈ WEDNESDAY ≈

## *Wednesday Morning Prayer*

### Opening Sentence

Her hands steadied the first steps
of him who steadied the earth to walk upon;
her lips helped the Word of God
to form his first human words.

### Canticle

God chose to be our mother in all things
      and so made the foundation of this work,
        most humbly and most pure, in the virgin's womb.
God the perfect wisdom of all
      was arrayed in this humble place.
Christ came in our poor flesh
      to share a mother's care.
Our mothers bore us for pain and for death;
      our true mother, Jesus, bears us for joy and endless life.
Christ carried us within him in love and travail,
      until the full time of his passion.

And when all was completed
and he had carried us so for joy,
still all this could not satisfy
the power of his wonderful love.


**Psalm 138**

I will give thanks to you, O God, with my whole heart;
before the gods I will sing your praise.

I will bow down toward your holy temple and praise your Name,
because of your love and faithfulness.

For you have glorified your Name
and your word above all things.

When I called, you answered me;
you increased my strength within me.

All the kings of the earth will praise you, O God,
when they have heard the words of your mouth.

They will sing of the ways of God,
that great is the glory of the Most High.

Though you are high, you care for the lowly;
you perceive the haughty from afar.

Though I walk in the midst of trouble, you keep me safe;
you stretch forth your hand against the fury of my enemies;
your right hand shall save me.

You will make good your purpose for me;
your love endures for ever;
do not abandon the works of your hands.

## Doxology

Glory to God, our Creator,
to God's most Holy Word,
and to the Spirit, indwelling;
as it was in the beginning,
is now and will be for ever.

## Scripture Reading

After eight days had passed, it was time to circumcise the child;
and he was called Jesus, the name given by the angel before he
was conceived in the womb.

When the time came for their purification according to the
law of Moses, they brought him up to Jerusalem to present him to
the Lord (as it is written in the law of the Lord, "Every firstborn
male shall be designated as holy to the Lord"), and they offered
a sacrifice according to what is stated in the law of the Lord, "a
pair of turtledoves or two young pigeons." . . . When they had
finished everything required by the law of the Lord, they returned
to Galilee, to their own town of Nazareth. The child grew and
became strong, filled with wisdom; and the favor of God was
upon him. *(Luke 2:21-24, 39–40)*

## Meditation

Mary saw, with a God-given clarity, at the moment of her greatest
crisis, that servanthood lies at the very centre of the meaning of
life as God intends it to be lived. Servanthood, obedience, in the
great crises of life and in the little decisions of everyday, Mary
saw as things of first importance. And so she doubtless taught the
little boy on her lap, at her knee, through all his formative years.

What greater prayer could she offer for her son than that he might grow up to be a servant of the Lord—possibly (did she glimpse it as she pondered on these things in her heart?) he might be even *the* servant of the Lord.

One of the greatest gifts that a mother can give to her children is not only to pray for them but, from their earliest years, to teach them to pray. We may be sure that Mary's little boy was not very old when he began to pray the prayer which his mother used when first she knew she was pregnant: 'I am the Lord's servant; may it be to me as you have said,' or, to put it more simply and shortly, 'Your will be done.'

## The Lord's Prayer

Our Father in heaven,
    hallowed be your Name,
    your kingdom come
    your will be done,
        on earth as in heaven.

Give us today our daily bread.

Forgive us our sins
    as we forgive those
        who sin against us.

Save us from the time of trial,
    and deliver us from evil.

For the kingdom, the power,
    and the glory are yours,
    now and for ever.  Amen.

**Prayer**

Holy One, who has loved us from our first cry to this day and this hour, help us to find within ourselves the nurture and tenderness you have for all creation. Help us to be your mothering love for our beautiful and strife-torn planet. We ask this in the name of him who was once a child of this earth. Amen.

**Blessing**

May Mary—honored in so many places
in great cathedrals and in lowly grass—
may she bless you and keep you.
May the Morning Star shine gently on your face
and the Evening Star show you your way home.
May the Star of the Sea guide you
across life's stormy waters
till you find safe harbour
and peace for your souls at the last.
Amen.

## *Wednesday Noon Prayer*

### Opening Sentence

We praise your child and likewise hymn you
as a living temple, Theotokos;
for the Lord who holds all things in his hand
dwelt within your womb,
and hallowed and glorified you,
and taught all to cry to you.

### Canticle

Because it was a woman
who built a house for death
a shining girl tore it down.
So now
when you ask for blessings
seek the supreme one
in the form of a woman
surpassing all that God made,
since in her
(O tender! O blessed!)
he became one of us.

### Psalm 119:97–103

Oh, how I love your law!
all the day long it is in my mind.

Your commandment has made me wiser than my enemies,
and it is always with me.

I have more understanding than all my teachers,
>    for your decrees are my study.

I am wiser than the elders,
>    because I observe your commandments.

I restrain my feet from every evil way,
>    that I may keep your word.

I do not shrink from your judgments,
>    because you yourself have taught me.

How sweet are your words to my taste!
>    they are sweeter than honey to my mouth.

## Doxology

Glory be to God,
who made us;
who bears our pain;
and who loves us;
as it was in the beginning,
is now, and will be for ever.  Amen.

## Scripture Reading

Now every year his parents went to Jerusalem for the festival of the Passover. And when he was twelve years old, they went up as usual for the festival. When the festival was ended and they started to return, the boy Jesus stayed behind in Jerusalem, but his parents did not know it. Assuming that he was in the group of travelers, they went a day's journey. Then they started to look for him among their relatives and friends. When they did not find him, they returned to Jerusalem to search for him. After three days they found him in the temple, sitting among the teachers, listening to them and asking them questions. And all who heard him were amazed at his understanding and his answers. When his parents saw him they were astonished; and his mother said to him, "Child, why have you treated us like this? Look, your father and I have been searching for you in great anxiety." He said to them, "Why were you searching for me? Did you not know that I must be in my Father's house?" But they did not understand what he said to them. Then he went down with them and came to Nazareth, and was obedient to them. His mother treasured all these things in her heart. *(Luke 2:41–51)*

## Meditation

Let me begin by saying that there is only one way in which we can pray and that is to pray with the heart. By the heart I mean the innermost core of the personality. It cannot be described but I think the reader will understand what I mean. Call it the will or the desire if you like. But, you will say, surely we can pray with the lips. No, we can't. Or with the eyes, looking at icons, for example. Again, no. Or with the ears, listening to the choir singing an anthem? No, once again. Or with the touch such as when we finger rosary beads? Absolutely not. Let me repeat: there is only one way to pray and that is with the heart. The lips, the eyes and the ears, the nose and the touch, may be a great help to prayer because, and only because, they help to move the heart.

## The Lord's Prayer

Our heavenly Father, hallowed is your name.
Your Kingdom is come. Your will is done,
    as in heaven so also on earth.
Give us the bread for our daily need.
And leave us serene,
    just as we also allowed others serenity.
And do not pass us through trial,
    except separate us from the evil one.
For yours is the Kingdom,
    the Power and the Glory
to the end of the universe, of all the universes.  Amen!

## Prayer

Spirit of God, you search us out and know us; you echo our questioning and set us dreaming on the vastness of this universe and the unfathomable secrets of ourselves. Direct our thinking this day, that we may do so with the mind in the heart, with intellect informed by affection. May we, like Mary, ponder you in our hearts. May we, like her, grow in grace and understanding, until on the last day our souls are fully realized and we rest, at last, in the mind of Christ.  Amen.

## Blessing

Go calmly in peace, for you will have a good escort, because He who created you has sent you the Holy Spirit and has always guarded you as a mother does her child who loves her.

# *Wednesday Evening Prayer*

## Opening Sentence

Sing we of the joys of Mary at whose breast the child was fed
who is Son of God eternal and the everlasting Bread.

## Canticle

My breath, my heart, my mind, my whole life fills with joy
        because of God, who's not forgotten me, whose strength
            surrounds and lifts me up.
All through the centuries that have passed
        God showed his patience and forgiveness;
God makes the proud and pompous folk look foolish,
        and cares for the simple ones who trust him.
God turns the rich and selfish into beggars.
        God feeds the hungry and the poor.
All through the centuries, God is faithful
        to those he promises will be his friends.
Your beauty fills the earth and the sky;
        the saints and angels sing to you;
God everlasting,
        Father, Son and Holy Spirit.

## Psalm 85

You have been gracious to your land, O God,
        you have restored the good fortune of Jacob.

You have forgiven the iniquity of your people
        and blotted out all their sins.

You have withdrawn all your fury
  and turned yourself from your wrathful indignation.

Restore us then, O God our Savior;
  let your anger depart from us.

Will you be displeased with us for ever?
  will you prolong your anger from age to age?

Will you not give us life again,
  that your people may rejoice in you?

Show us your mercy, O God,
  and grant us your salvation.

I will listen to what you are saying,
  for you are speaking peace to your faithful people
  and to those who turn their hearts to you.

Truly, your salvation is very near to those who fear you,
  that your glory may dwell in our land.

Mercy and truth have met together;
  righteousness and peace have kissed each other.

Truth shall spring up from the earth,
  and righteousness shall look down from heaven.

God will indeed grant prosperity,
  and our land will yield its increase.

Righteousness shall go before you,
  and peace shall be a pathway for your feet.

## Doxology

Glory to God, Source of all being,
Eternal Word, and Holy Spirit;
as it was in the beginning, is now
and will be for ever.  Amen.

## Scripture Reading

A shoot shall come out from the stump of Jesse,
      and a branch shall grow out of his roots.
The spirit of the LORD shall rest on him,
      the spirit of wisdom and understanding,
      the spirit of counsel and might,
      the spirit of knowledge and fear of the LORD.
His delight shall be in the fear of the LORD.
He shall not judge by what his eyes see,
      or decide by what his ears hear;
but with righteousness he shall judge the poor,
      and decide with equity for the meek of the earth;
he shall strike the earth with the rod of his mouth,
      and with the breath of his lips he shall kill the wicked.
Righteousness shall be the belt around his waist,
      and faithfulness the belt around his loins.
The wolf shall live with the lamb,
      the leopard shall lie down with the kid,
the calf and the lion and the fatling together,
      and a little child shall lead them. *(Isaiah 11:1–6)*

## Meditation

When Jesus was in Bethany in the house of Simon the leper, a woman anointed his head with costly ointment as he sat at table. When his disciples muttered about the waste, Jesus said, "She has done a beautiful thing to me. . . Truly, I say to you, wherever this gospel is preached in the whole world, what she has done will be told in memory of her" (Mt 26:10,13). If such a simple act was worth remembering for ever, how much more worth remembering is the mothering Jesus received from Mary?

## The Lord's Prayer

Eternal Spirit,
Pain-bearer, Love-maker, Life-giver,
Source of all that is and that shall be,
Father and Mother of us all,
Loving God, in whom is heaven:

The hallowing of your name echo through the universe!
The way of your justice be followed by the peoples of the world!
Your heavenly will be done by all created beings!
Your commonwealth of peace and freedom sustain our hope and come on earth.

With the bread we need for today, feed us.
In the hurts we absorb from one another, forgive us.
In times of temptation and test, strengthen us.
From trials too great to endure, spare us.
From the grip of all that is evil, free us.
For you reign in the glory of the power that is love, now and for ever. Amen.

## Prayer

O God, the source of all insight,
whose coming was revealed to the nations
not among men of power
but on a woman's lap:
give us grace to seek you
where you may be found,
that the wisdom of this world may be humbled
and discover your unexpected joy,
through Jesus Christ.  Amen.

## Blessing

Father of lights,
from whom comes every good and perfect gift;
Mother of lights,
from whom comes our best insight and inspiration:
Help us to find you in stars and seasons, in darkness and silence,
in love and longing, and to bless your holy name.
Amen.

## *Wednesday Night Prayer*

### Opening Sentence

As many roads to God there are
As his children have breaths,
But, of all the roads to God,
Mary's Way is the sweetest and the gentlest.

## Canticle

Holy Mary, pray for us.

Mother of our Savior, pray for us.

Mother who said a clear "yes" to God, pray for us.

Mother who journeyed to share your joy, pray for us.

Mother who treasured God's word in your heart, pray for us.

Mother who bore your firstborn in a stable, pray for us.

Mother who fled with your infant to Egypt, pray for us.

Mother who watched your child grow in wisdom, pray for us.

Mother who lost your young boy for three days, pray for us.

Mother who pondered God's ways in your heart, pray for us.

Mother who prompted the miracle at Cana, pray for us.

Mother who followed your son on his journey, pray for us.

Mother who became his faithful disciple, pray for us.

Mother who walked the sad road to Calvary, pray for us.

Mother who stood at the foot of the cross, pray for us.

Mother who held your dead child in your arms, pray for us.

Mother who beheld your son risen as promised, pray for us.

Mother who rejoiced as the Spirit descended, pray for us.

Holy Mary, pray for us.

Mother of God, pray for us.

Holy Mary, pray for us,

this day and always.  Amen.

## Psalm 24:1–6

The earth is God's and all that is in it,
>    the world and all who dwell therein.

For it is God who founded it upon the seas
>    and made it firm upon the rivers of the deep.

"Who can ascend the hill of the Holy One?
>    and who can stand in God's holy place?"

"Those who have clean hands and a pure heart,
>    who have not pledged themselves to falsehood,
>    nor sworn by what is a fraud.

They shall receive a blessing from the Most High
>    and a just reward from the God of their salvation."

Such is the generation of those who seek you,
>    of those who seek your face, O God of Jacob.

## Doxology

Glory be to the Father, and to the Son, and to the Holy Spirit:
as it was in the beginning, is now, and will be for ever. Amen.

## Scripture Reading

On the third day there was a wedding in Cana of Galilee, and the mother of Jesus was there. Jesus and his disciples had also been invited to the wedding. When the wine gave out, the mother of Jesus said to him, "They have no wine." And Jesus said to her, "Woman, what concern is that to you and to me? My hour has not yet come." His mother said to the servants, "Do whatever he tells you." Now standing there were six stone water jars for the Jewish rites of purification, each holding twenty or thirty gallons. Jesus said to them, "Fill the jars with water." And they filled them up to the brim. He said to them, "Now draw some out, and take it to the chief steward." So they took it. When the steward tasted the water that had become wine, and did not know where it came from (though the servants who had drawn the water knew), the steward called the bridegroom and said to him, "Everyone serves the good wine first, and then the inferior wine after the guests have become drunk. But you have kept the good wine until now." Jesus did this, the first of his signs, in Cana of Galilee, and revealed his glory; and his disciples believed in him. *(John 2:1–11)*

### Meditation

Because she must have known
    how the glimmer in blue shadows
        becomes the flight of swallows;

how the long limbs of moonlight
    make mystery welcome;
        how wonder is a kind of manna.

It was, after all, her idea.
    She had seen the hour flagging.
        Why else would she insist?

She knew how a moment turned back
    with a halt or refusal
        and all of life turned with it.

She knew also how eternity surfaced,
    how light-reflecting water
        could sweeten in our mouths to wine.

## The Lord's Prayer

Our Father, who art in heaven,
hallowed be thy Name,
thy kingdom come,
thy will be done,
on earth as it is in heaven.

Give us this day our daily bread.

And forgive us our trespasses,
as we forgive those
who trespass against us.

And lead us not into temptation,
but deliver us from evil.

For thine is the kingdom,
and the power, and the glory,
for ever and ever.  Amen.

## Prayer

Christ our Lord, help us to follow your mother Mary's directive, and do whatever you tell us to do. Give us faith that your will for us leads to the fullness of life, and that if we will but entrust our whole lives to you, water will be turned into wine, sorrow into dancing, and death into everlasting life.  Amen.

## Blessing

Christ stands before you, and peace is in his mind.
Sleep in the calm of all calm,
sleep in the guidance of all guidance,
sleep in the love of all loves,
sleep, beloved, in the God of life.

# ❧ THURSDAY ☙

## *Thursday Morning Prayer*

### Opening Sentence

Before the sun comes up,
we, your children of Africa,
want to praise you joyfully, Mary.
You are black but beautiful. . .
We love you more than the
drum music of the evenings.

### Canticle

My soul rejoices in the Lord,
My spirit leaps before my God and savior,
Who favors his waiting servant.
Listen!
From now on, everyone will call me happy!
For the heavens did great things unto me,
Holy is his name.
From this time and forever,
Mercy flows to those who fear him.

His strong arm spread,
He scatters the thoughts of arrogant hearts,
He snatches the powerful from high places.
And lifts up the empty.
The hungry are fed delicious food
And the rich sent away with nothing.
His child Israel is clothed in forgiveness,
Just as he spoke to our fathers,
Abraham and his seed forever.

## Psalm 1

Happy are they who have not walked in the counsel of the wicked,
>    nor lingered in the way of sinners,
>    nor sat in the seats of the scornful!

Their delight is in the law of the Most High,
>    and they meditate on that law day and night.

They are like trees planted by streams of water,
>    bearing fruit in due season, with leaves that do not wither;
>    everything they do shall prosper.

It is not so with the wicked;
>    they are like chaff which the wind blows away.

Therefore the wicked shall not stand upright
>    when judgment comes,
>    nor the sinner in the council of the righteous.

For God knows the way of the righteous,
>    but the way of the wicked is doomed.

## Doxology

Glory to God, Source of all being,
Eternal Word, and Holy Spirit;
as it was in the beginning, is now
and will be for ever. Amen.

## Scripture Reading

Then he looked up at his disciples and said:
"Blessed are you who are poor, for yours is the kingdom of God.
Blessed are you who are hungry now, for you will be filled.
Blessed are you who weep now, for you will laugh. Blessed are
you when people hate you, and when they exclude you, revile
you, and defame you on account of the Son of Man. Rejoice in
that day and leap for joy, for surely your reward is great in heaven;
for that is what their ancestors did to the prophets. But woe to
you who are rich, for you have received your consolation. Woe to
you who are full now, for you will be hungry. Woe to you who are
laughing now, for you will mourn and weep. Woe to you when all
speak well of you, for that is what their ancestors did to the false
prophets." *(Luke 6:20–26)*

## Meditation

Whoever, therefore, would show her the proper honor must not
regard her alone and by herself, but set her in the presence of God
and far beneath Him, must there strip her of all honor, and regard
her low estate, as she says; he should then marvel at the exceed-
ing abundant grace of God who regards, embraces, and blesses
so poor and despised a mortal. Thus regarding her, you will be
moved to love and praise God for His grace, and drawn to look

for all good things to Him, who does not reject but graciously regards poor and despised and lowly mortals. Thus your heart will be strengthened in faith and love and hope. What do you suppose would please her more than to have you come through her to God this way, and learn from her to put your hope and trust in Him, notwithstanding your despised and lowly estate, in life as well as in death? She does not want you to come to her, but through her to God. Again, nothing would please her better than to have you turn in fear from all lofty things on which men set their hearts, seeing that even in His mother God neither found nor desired anything of high degree.

**The Lord's Prayer**

Our Father in heaven,
  hallowed be your Name,
  your kingdom come,
  your will be done,
    on earth as in heaven.

Give us today our daily bread.

Forgive us our sins
  as we forgive those
    who sin against us.

Save us from the time of trial,
  and deliver us from evil.

For the kingdom, the power,
  and the glory are yours,
  now and for ever. Amen.

**Prayer**

Holy One, we give you thanks for this new day that stretches light and white as canvas before us. Give us wisdom to behold this morning as the gift it is; as hours and minutes full of possibilities, as one of a decreasing number of our days on earth, as a day in which we can become the person you would have us be. Help us to spread abroad your generous love and forgive our enemies, that our prayer this night may be thanksgiving for your amazing grace. We pray in the name of the Holy Spirit, who with you and your Christ lives and reigns, now and forever. Amen.

**Blessing**

May God the Holy Spirit,
by whose working the Virgin Mary conceived the Christ,
help us bear the fruits of holiness. Amen.

# *Thursday Noon Prayer*

## Opening Sentence

First look upon the face
That most resembles Christ's
For only the beauty of her face
Can prepare thee to see
The face of Christ.

## Canticle

The earth is at the same time mother.
She is mother of all that is natural,
mother of all that is human.

She is the mother of all,
for contained in her are the seeds of all.

The earth of humankind contains all moistness,
all verdancy,
all germinating power.

It is in so many ways fruitful.

All creation comes from it,
yet it forms not only the basic raw material for humankind
but also the substance of the incarnation of God's Son.

## Psalm 1

Happy are they who have not walked in the counsel of the wicked,
    nor lingered in the way of sinners,
    nor sat in the seats of the scornful!

Their delight is in the law of the Most High,
    and they meditate on that law day and night.

They are like trees planted by streams of water,
    bearing fruit in due season, with leaves that do not wither;
    everything they do shall prosper.

It is not so with the wicked;
    they are like chaff which the wind blows away.

Therefore the wicked shall not stand upright
        when judgment comes,
    nor the sinner in the council of the righteous.

For God knows the way of the righteous,
    but the way of the wicked is doomed.

## Doxology

Glory be to the Father, and to the Son, and to the Holy Spirit:
as it was in the beginning, is now, and will be for ever. Amen.

## Scripture Reading

While he was still speaking to the crowds, his mother and his
brothers were standing outside, wanting to speak to him. Someone
told him, "Look, your mother and your brothers are standing outside, wanting to speak to you." But to the one who had told him
this, Jesus replied, "Who is my mother, and who are my brothers?"

And pointing to his disciples, he said, "Here are my mother and my brothers! For whoever does the will of my Father in heaven is my brother and sister and mother." *(Matthew 12:46–50)*

## Meditation

The blessedness of the holy Virgin is not so altogether proper to her, or incommunicable to others, but that the meanest sincere Christian may share with her in the better part of it. Wonderful and full of comfort are the words of our Saviour, Luke xi. Where, when a certain woman, hearing his excellent discourse, cried out, *Blessed is the womb that bare thee, and the paps which thou hast sucked,* our Saviour answers, *Yea rather, blessed are they that hear the word of God and keep it.* Which is not a negation of the blessedness of his mother, (for that would be a plain contradiction to my text,) but a correction of the woman's mistake, who so admired the blessedness of the mother of such a son, that she scarce thought of any other blessedness. Our Saviour therefore tells her, that *blessed are they also, yea and chiefly, that hear the word of God, and keep it.*

## The Lord's Prayer

Our Father, who art in heaven,
> hallowed be thy Name,
> thy kingdom come
> thy will be done,
>> on earth as it is in heaven.

Give us this day our daily bread.

And forgive us our trespasses,
    as we forgive those
        who trespass against us.

And lead us not into temptation,
    but deliver us from evil.

For thine is the kingdom,
    and the power, and the glory,
    for ever and ever.  Amen.


**Prayer**

Forgiving God,
your Son once said
that his brother, sister, mother
were all who did your will.
Yet even when we fail to do your will
you welcome and accept us
as your children.
Teach us to include others
as readily as you include us;
for to do so is your heavenly will.
Amen.


**Blessing**

The blessing of God, the eternal goodwill of God, the shalom
of God, the wildness and the warmth of God, be among us and
between us, now and always.  Amen.

## *Thursday Evening Prayer*

### Opening Sentence

The spirit of the Lord GOD is upon me,
because the LORD has anointed me;
he has sent me to bring good news to the oppressed. *(Isaiah 61:1)*

### Canticle

Hail, O Lady, holy Queen,
Mary, holy Mother of God:
you are the Virgin made Church,
and the one chosen by the most holy Father in heaven
whom he consecrated with his most holy beloved Son
and with the Holy Spirit the Paraclete,
in whom there was and is
all the fullness of grace and every good.
Hail, his Palace!
Hail, his Tabernacle!
Hail, his Home!
Hail, his Robe!
Hail, his Servant!
Hail, his Mother!
And hail all you holy virtues
which through the grace and light of the Holy Spirit
are poured into the hearts of the faithful
so that from their faithless state
you may make them faithful to God.  Amen.

## Psalm 23

God is my shepherd;
>I shall not be in want.

You make me lie down in green pastures
>and lead me beside still waters.

You revive my soul
>and guide me along right pathways for your Name's sake.

Though I walk through the valley of the shadow of death,
>I shall fear no evil;
>>for you are with me; your rod and your staff,
>>>they comfort me.

You spread a table before me in the presence
>of those who trouble me;
>you have anointed my head with oil,
>>and my cup is running over.

Surely your goodness and mercy shall follow me
>all the days of my life,
>and I will dwell in the house of the Most High for ever.

## Doxology

Glory to God, our Creator,
to God's most Holy Word,
and to the Spirit, indwelling;
as it was in the beginning,
is now and will be for ever.  Amen.

## Scripture Reading

One of the Pharisees asked Jesus to eat with him, and he went into the Pharisee's house and took his place at the table. And a woman in the city, who was a sinner, having learned that he was eating in the Pharisee's house, brought an alabaster jar of ointment. She stood behind him at his feet, weeping, and began to bathe his feet with her tears and to dry them with her hair. Then she continued kissing his feet and anointing them with the ointment.

Turning toward the woman, [Jesus] said to Simon, "Do you see this woman? I entered your house; you gave me no water for my feet, but she has bathed my feet with her tears and dried them with her hair. You gave me no kiss, but from the time I came in she has not stopped kissing my feet. You did not anoint my head with oil, but she has anointed my feet with ointment. Therefore, I tell you, her sins, which were many, have been forgiven; hence she has shown great love. But the one to whom little is forgiven, loves little." *(Luke 7:36–38, 44–47)*

## Meditation

My hair, dark, copper in sunlight
grows thick and curling in the fog.
I prized it, knew it could excite
husbands to break the Decalog.

Tonight I use it as a towel
to dry a pair of tear-washed feet.
It is my way toward an avowal
to end my living on the street.

These curls now consecrate with oil
but touch the foot and not the head.
I mingle ritual with my toil,
as kings are ordained and the dead.

I bind my hair, now wet and mussed,
heavy with unction, mercy, dust.


## The Lord's Prayer

Our Father in heaven,
Reveal who you are.
Set the world right;
Do what's best—
        as above, so below.
Keep us alive with three square meals.
Keep us forgiven with you and forgiving others.
Keep us safe from ourselves and the Devil.


## Prayer

God our Father,
you chose Mary from the lowly among your people,
and her one desire was to be your handmaid.
Through her intercession,
grant us poverty of spirit,
and reveal to us the mysteries of your kingdom,
through Jesus, the Christ, our Lord.  Amen.

## Blessing

May God the Holy Spirit shed her radiance upon the earth this night, blessing all who seek to serve her, renewing our hopes, entering our souls, and making us friends with God. Amen.

## *Thursday Night Prayer*

### Opening Sentence

Magnify, my soul, God's greatness; in my Savior I rejoice;
all the ages call me blessed, in his praise I lift my voice;
he has cast down all the mighty, and the lowly are his choice.

### Canticle

O Mary don't you weep, don't you mourn
O Mary don't you weep, don't you mourn
Pharaoh's army got drownded
O Mary don't you weep.
Well Mary wore three links and chains
On every link was Jesus' name
Pharaoh's army got drownded
O Mary don't you weep.

O Mary don't you weep, don't you mourn
O Mary don't you weep, don't you mourn
Pharaoh's army got drownded
O Mary don't you weep.

## Psalm 8

O Most High, our Sovereign,
>how exalted is your Name in all the world!

Out of the mouths of infants and children
>your majesty is praised above the heavens.

You have set up a stronghold against your adversaries,
>to quell the enemy and the avenger.

When I consider your heavens, the work of your fingers,
>the moon and the stars you have set in their courses,

What are we that you should be mindful of us?
>your children that you should seek us out?

You have made us but little lower than the angels;
>you adorn us with glory and honor.

You give us mastery over the works of your hands,
>you put all things under our feet:

All sheep and oxen,
>even the wild beasts of the field,

The birds of the air, the fish of the sea,
>and whatsoever walks in the paths of the sea.

O Most High, our Sovereign,
>how exalted is your Name in all the world!

## Doxology

Glory be to God,
who made us;
who bears our pain;
and who loves us;
as it was in the beginning,
is now, and will be for ever.  Amen.


## Scripture Reading

While they were eating, Jesus took a loaf of bread, and after blessing it he broke it, gave it to the disciples, and said, "Take, eat; this is my body." Then he took a cup, and after giving thanks he gave it to them, saying, "Drink from it, all of you; for this is my blood of the covenant, which is poured out for many for the forgiveness of sins. I tell you, I will never again drink of this fruit of the vine until that day when I drink it new with you in my Father's kingdom." *(Matthew 26:26–29)*


## Meditation

Our Lady is our mother, in whom we are all enclosed and born of her in Christ, for she who is mother of our saviour is mother of all who are saved in our saviour; and our saviour is our true Mother, in whom we are endlessly born and out of whom we shall never come.

We know that all our mothers bear us for pain and death. But our true Mother Jesus bears us for joy and for endless life, blessed may he be. The mother can give her child to suck of her milk, but our precious Mother Jesus can feed us with himself, and does, most courteously and tenderly, with the blessed sacrament.

**The Lord's Prayer**

Seed and source,
      far in the distance and in our souls,
      you are holy and make us whole.

May we perceive your divine will
      that loved us into being.

Help us to join your creative force
      and let it prosper here.

Give us what we need to survive,
      and release us from our transgressions,
      as we release others from theirs.

Keep us from the paths of destruction
      and from those who would ruin what you have made,
      for you are the matrix of life, love, and wisdom,
      now and forever.  Amen.

**Prayer**

Christ our brother, whose blessed mother placed you in a feeding trough because she had no cradle; you who would later come to see your own body as nourishment for us all: give to us, your followers, grace to reach out to others and to all of creation in love and service, that your kingdom may be on earth as it is in heaven. We ask this of you, the Source of salvation, who with the Source of being and Source of transformation, gives us life in its fullness, now and always.  Amen.

## Blessing

The deep peace of the saints be with you tonight.
The deep peace of Mary be with you tonight.
The deep peace of Jesus be with you tonight.
The deep peace of the Spirit be with you tonight.
The deep peace of your Creator be with you tonight,
circling you and those you love in this blessing of peace.
Amen.

# ~ FRIDAY ~

## *Friday Morning Prayer*

### Opening Sentence

What, do you wish to know your Lord's meaning in this thing?
Know it well, love was his meaning.

### Canticle

How beautiful upon the mountains
>   are the feet of the messenger who announces peace,
who brings good news,
>   who announces salvation,
>   who says to Zion, "Your God reigns."

Listen! Your sentinels lift up their voices,
>   together they sing for joy;
for in plain sight they see
>   the return of the LORD to Zion.

Break forth together into singing,
>   you ruins of Jerusalem;
for the LORD has comforted his people,
>   he has redeemed Jerusalem.

See, my servant shall prosper;
>> he shall be exalted and lifted up,
>> and shall be very high.

Just as there were many who were astonished at him
>> —so marred was his appearance,
>>> beyond human semblance,
>> and his form beyond that of mortals—

so shall he startle many nations;
>> kings shall shut their mouths because of him;

for that which had not been told them they shall see,
>> and that which they had not heard
>> they shall contemplate. *(Isaiah 52:7–9, 13–15)*

## Psalm 130

Out of the depths have I called to you; O God, hear my voice;
>> let your ears consider well the voice of my supplication.

If you were to note what is done amiss,
>> O God, who could stand?

For there is forgiveness with you;
>> therefore you shall be feared.

I wait for you, O God; my soul waits for you;
>> in your word is my hope.

My soul waits for you, more than the night-watch for the morning,
>> more than the night-watch for the morning.

O Israel, wait for God,
>for with our God there is mercy;

With you there is plenteous redemption,
>and you will redeem Israel from all their sins.

## Doxology

Glory be to the Father, and to the Son, and to the Holy Spirit:
as it was in the beginning, is now, and will be for ever. Amen.

## Scripture Reading

He came out and went, as was his custom, to the Mount of Olives; and the disciples followed him. When he reached the place, he said to them, "Pray that you may not come into the time of trial." Then he withdrew from them about a stone's throw, knelt down, and prayed, "Father, if you are willing, remove this cup from me; yet, not my will but yours be done." Then an angel from heaven appeared to him and gave him strength. In his anguish he prayed more earnestly, and his sweat became like great drops of blood falling down on the ground. When he got up from prayer, he came to the disciples and found them sleeping because of grief, and he said to them, "Why are you sleeping? Get up and pray that you may not come into the time of trial." *(Luke 22:39–46)*

## Meditation

"Praise, praise!" I croak. Praise God for all that's holy, cold, and dark. Praise him for all we lose, for all the river of the years bears off. Praise him for stillness in the wake of pain. Praise him for emptiness. And as you race to spill into the sea, praise him yourself, old [River] Wear. Praise him for dying and the peace of death.

In the little church I built of wood for Mary, I hollowed out a place for him. Perkin brings him by the pail and pours him in. Now that I can hardly walk, I crawl to meet him there. He takes me in his chilly lap to wash me of my sins. Or I kneel down beside him till within his depths I see a star.

Sometimes this star is still. Sometimes she dances. She is Mary's star. Within that little pool of Wear she winks at me. I wink at her. The secret that we share I cannot tell in full. But this much I will tell. What's lost is nothing to what's found, and all the death that ever was, set next to life, would scarcely fill a cup.

## The Lord's Prayer

Our Father, who art in heaven,
> hallowed be thy Name,
> thy kingdom come,
> thy will be done,
>> on earth as it is in heaven.

Give us this day our daily bread.

And forgive us our trespasses,
> as we forgive those
>> who trespass against us.

And lead us not into temptation,
> but deliver us from evil.

For thine is the kingdom,
> and the power, and the glory,
> for ever and ever.  Amen.

**Prayer**

Almighty God, whom we are called to love with our whole heart, mind, soul, and with a bold strength: we know well that we are often heartless toward the misery of others and mindless toward thy purposes for good, that our souls wither among our machines, that our strength has gone from us laboring after that which does not satisfy. By our luxury the hungry are sent empty away; for the sake of our comfort the innocent perish at home and abroad. As of old, we kill the prophets and anoint the fools. Help us, great Lord, to deplore in ourselves the evil that so wantonly destroys; and provoke in us for the sake of all people those inward changes which support life, encourage liberty, and make possible the pursuit of happiness. Amen.

**Blessing**

May the most holy Mother of God intercede for us with the Lord. Amen.

# *Friday Noon Prayer*

## Opening Sentence

Who is that fine man upon the Passion Tree?
It is your son, dear Mother, know you not me?

## Psalm 27:5–11

One thing have I asked of the Most High; one thing I seek;
>that I may dwell in the house of God all the days of my life;

To behold the fair beauty of God
>and to seek you in your temple.

For in the day of trouble you will keep me safe in your shelter;
>you will hide me in the secrecy of your dwelling
>and set me high upon a rock.

Even now you lift up my head
>above my enemies round about me.

Therefore I will offer in your dwelling an oblation
with sounds of great gladness;
>I will sing and make music to you, O God.

Hearken to my voice when I call;
>have mercy on me and answer me.

You speak in my heart and say, "Seek my face."
>Your face, O God, will I seek.

## Doxology

Glory be to God,
who made us;
who bears our pain;
and who loves us;
as it was in the beginning,
is now, and will be for ever. Amen.

## Scripture Reading

Let the same mind be in you that was in Christ Jesus,
who, though he was in the form of God,
did not regard equality with God
as something to be exploited,
but emptied himself,
taking the form of a slave,
being born in human likeness.
And being found in human form,
he humbled himself
and became obedient to the point of death—
even death on a cross.

Therefore God also highly exalted him
and gave him the name
that is above every name,
so that at the name of Jesus
every knee should bend,
in heaven and on earth and under the earth,
and every tongue should confess
that Jesus Christ is Lord,
to the glory of God the Father. *(Philippians 2:5–11)*

## Meditation

Seeing her own Lamb led to the slaughter, Mary His Mother followed him with the other women and in her grief she cried: "Where dost Thou go, my Child? Why dost Thou run so swiftly? Is there another wedding in Cana, and art Thou hastening there, to turn the water into wine? Shall I go with Thee, my Child, or shall I wait for Thee? Speak some word to me, O Word; do not pass me by in silence."

## The Lord's Prayer

Our Father in heaven,
> hallowed be your Name,
> your kingdom come,
> your will be done,
>> on earth as in heaven.

Give us today our daily bread.

Forgive us our sins
> as we forgive those
>> who sin against us.

Save us from the time of trial,
> and deliver us from evil.

For the kingdom, the power,
> and the glory are yours,
> now and for ever.  Amen.

**The Angelus**

*The Angel of the Lord announced to Mary, and she conceived by the Holy Spirit.*

Hail Mary, full of grace, the Lord is with you. Blessed are you among women, and blessed is the fruit of your womb, Jesus.

Holy Mary, Mother of God, pray for us sinners, now and at the hour of our death. Amen.

*I am the handmaid of the Lord; let it be with me according to your word.*

Hail Mary, full of grace, the Lord is with you. Blessed are you among women, and blessed is the fruit of your womb, Jesus.

Holy Mary, Mother of God, pray for us sinners, now and at the hour of our death. Amen.

*And the Word was made Flesh and lived among us.*

Hail Mary, full of grace, the Lord is with you. Blessed are you among women, and blessed is the fruit of your womb, Jesus.

Holy Mary, Mother of God, pray for us sinners, now and at the hour of our death. Amen.

*Pray for us, O holy Mother of God,*
*that we may be made worthy of the promises of Christ.*

### Prayer

Pour your grace into our hearts, O Lord, that we who have known the incarnation of your Son Jesus Christ, announced by an angel to the Virgin Mary, may by his cross and passion be brought to the glory of his resurrection; who lives and reigns with you, in the unity of the Holy Spirit, one God, now and for ever. Amen.

### Blessing

Crucified Savior, help us to hope and trust in the presence of your Blessed Mother when we carry our cross in your name. Amen.

## *Friday Evening Prayer*

### Opening Sentence

Through her we may see him
Made sweeter, not made dim,
And her hand leaves his light
Sifted to suit our sight.

### Canticle

Who would have believed what we have heard:
> and to whom has the power of the Lord been revealed?

He grew up before the Lord like a tender plant:
> like a root out of arid ground.

He had no beauty, no majesty to draw our eyes:
>> no grace to make us delight in him.

He was despised and rejected:
>> a man of sorrows and familiar with suffering.

Like one from whom people hide their faces:
>> he was despised and we esteemed him not.

Surely he has borne our griefs and carried our sorrows:
>> yet we considered him stricken,
>>> smitten by God, and afflicted.

But he was wounded for our transgressions:
>> he was bruised for our iniquities.

The punishment that brought us peace was laid upon him:
>> and by his wounds we are healed. *(Isaiah 53:1–5)*

## Psalm 22:1–11

My God my God, why have you forsaken me?
>> and are you so far from my cry, and words of my distress?

O my God I cry out in the daytime, but you do not answer;
>> at night as well, but I find no rest.

Yet you are the Holy One:
>> enthroned upon the praises of Israel.

Our forebears put their trust in you:
>> they trusted, and you delivered them.

They cried out to you and were delivered:
>> they trusted in you, and were not put to shame.

But as for me, I am a worm, a mere nothing
>> scorned by all and and despised by the people.

All those who see me laugh me to scorn:
>they curl their lips and toss their heads saying,

"You trusted in God; let God deliver you;
>and rescue you, if God delights in you."

Yet you are the one who took me out of the womb:
>you kept me safe upon my mother's breast.

I have been entrusted to you ever since I was born:
>you were my God when I was still in my mother's womb.

Be not far from me, for trouble is near,
>and there is none to help.

## Doxology

Glory to God, our Creator,
to God's most Holy Word,
and to the Spirit, indwelling;
as it was in the beginning,
is now and will be for ever.  Amen.

## Scripture Reading

Meanwhile, standing near the cross of Jesus were his mother, and his mother's sister, Mary the wife of Clopas, and Mary Magdalene. When Jesus saw his mother and the disciple whom he loved standing beside her, he said to his mother, "Woman, here is your son." Then he said to the disciple, "Here is your mother." And from that hour the disciple took her into his own home. *(John 19:25b–27)*

## Meditation

When the visitor told her
there would be a child
and that she would be
overshadowed by holiness
she felt the holy darkness
that would someday become
the bringer of light.

And thirty-four years later
she stood on a hill
beneath another shadow
a high cross-bar that cut
across her and she held in
the thin air and silence
the elongated and forsaken
shadow of the holy one
she once held as a child.

She wondered as the shadows
gave way into the night
if, in time, light could pierce
like tiny nails, this absorbing dark.

**The Lord's Prayer**

Holy One,
> we honor your name.

Let the world know your justice
> here as everywhere.

Give us the food we need
> both for the body and the soul.

Forgive us the wrongs we do
> as we forgive the wrongs of others.

Keep us safe from the evil
> at large or of our own making.

We trust you for you made us and
> we are yours, now and always. Amen.

**Prayer**

Blessed Jesus, we remember the grief you suffered when, like a common criminal, you were fastened to the cross and almost all of your followers abandoned you. Your mother stood close by you through your pain and you entrusted your faithful disciple to her care and your mother to his. For the sake of the sword of sorrow which pierced her, have compassion on those who now suffer, and remember us all at the hour of our death. Amen.

**Blessing**

Be present, O merciful God, and protect us through the hours of this night, so that we who are wearied by the changes and chances of this life may rest in your eternal changelessness; through Jesus Christ our Lord. Amen.

## *Friday Night Prayer*

### Opening Sentence

O come, O come, thou wisdom strange
from deep within God's womb to range,
the earth at midnight's hour of fears
to make us wise beyond our years.

### Canticle

My soul sings out the greatness of God;
>    my spirit grows great in the Source of the free,
>    for God has seen my humble hopes
>    and from this day forward all will call me happy,
>    for the Holy One has raised me up
>    and honored is that name.

God has heard all who cry to heaven for help
>    in every time and every place.

The Eternal has shown the might of righteousness
>    and sent the arrogant flying both in mind and heart.

The Sovereign has thrown down the powerful from high places
>    and lifted up the lowly poor;

The Creator has delighted the hungry with sweet meats
>    and left the rich an empty belly.

God has come to help those who serve the holy;
>    and remembers the promise of compassion,
>    the promise made to our mothers and fathers,
>    to the children of Sarah and Abraham forever.

## Psalm 13

How long, O God? will you forget me for ever?
> how long will you hide your face from me?

How long shall I have perplexity in my mind,
> and grief in my heart, day after day?
> how long shall my enemy triumph over me?

Look upon me and answer me, O God;
> give light to my eyes, lest I sleep in death,

Lest my enemy say, "I have prevailed over you,"
> and my foes rejoice that I have fallen.

But I put my trust in your mercy;
> my heart is joyful because of your saving help.

I will sing to my God who has dealt with me richly;
> I will praise the Name of God Most High.

## Doxology

Glory to God, Source of all being,
Eternal Word, and Holy Spirit;
as it was in the beginning, is now
and will be for ever. Amen.

## Scripture Reading

A great portent appeared in heaven: a woman clothed with the sun, with the moon under her feet, and on her head a crown of twelve stars. She was pregnant and was crying out in birthpangs, in the agony of giving birth. Then another portent appeared in heaven: a great red dragon, with seven heads and ten horns, and seven diadems on his heads. His tail swept down a third of the stars of heaven and threw them to the earth. Then the dragon stood before the woman who was about to bear a child, so that he might devour her child as soon as it was born. And she gave birth to a son, a male child, who is to rule all the nations with a rod of iron. But her child was snatched away and taken to God and to his throne; and the woman fled into the wilderness, where she has a place prepared by God. . . .

So when the dragon saw that he had been thrown down to the earth, he pursued the woman who had given birth to the male child. But the woman was given the two wings of the great eagle, so that she could fly from the serpent into the wilderness, to her place where she is nourished for a time, and times, and half a time. Then from his mouth the serpent poured water like a river after the woman, to sweep her away with the flood. But the earth came to the help of the woman; it opened its mouth and swallowed the river that the dragon had poured from his mouth. Then the dragon was angry with the woman, and went off to make war on the rest of her children, those who keep the commandments of God and hold the testimony of Jesus. *(Revelation 12:1–6,13–17)*

## Meditation

If everyone were holy and handsome, with *alter Christus* shining in neon lighting from them, it would be easy to see Christ in everyone. If Mary had appeared in Bethlehem clothed, as St. John says, with the sun, a crown of twelve stars on her heard, and the moon under her feet, then people would have fought to make room for her. But that was not God's way for her, nor is it Christ's way for himself, now when he is disguised under every type of humanity that treads the earth.

## The Lord's Prayer

Eternal Spirit,
Pain-bearer, Love-maker, Life-giver,
Source of all that is and that shall be,
Father and Mother of us all,
Loving God, in whom is heaven:

The hallowing of your name echo through the universe
The way of your justice be followed by the peoples of the world!

Your heavenly will be done by all created beings!

Your commonwealth of peace and freedom sustain our hope and
come on earth.
With the bread we need for today, feed us.
In the hurts we absorb from one another, forgive us.
In times of temptation and test, strengthen us.
From trials too great to endure, spare us.
From the grip of all that is evil, free us.
For you reign in the glory of the power that is love, now and
forever.  Amen.

**Prayer**

God our Sovereign,
when Jesus was dying for us
Mary his mother stood by his side,
in the darkness which covered the earth.
In the unending dawn of the resurrection,
may she stand as a sign of our sure hope,
that we will one day be with you,
the Light that will shine for ever and ever.  Amen.

**Blessing**

May the prayers of the woman clothed with the sun
bring Jesus to the waiting world
and fill the void of incompletion
with the presence of her child.
Amen.

# ❧ SATURDAY ❧

## *Saturday Morning Prayer*

### Opening Sentence

My son, my senses are wounded
And my heart is burned
As I see you dead!
Yet, trusting in your resurrection,
I magnify You!

### Canticle

Jesus, as a mother you gather your people to you;
> you are gentle with us as a mother with her children.

Often you weep over our sins and our pride;
> tenderly you draw us from hatred and judgment.

You comfort us in sorrow and bind up our wounds;
> in sickness you nurse us and with pure milk you feed us.

Jesus, by your dying we are born to new life;
> by your anguish and labor we come forth in joy.

Despair turns to hope through your sweet goodness;
> through your gentleness, we find comfort in fear.

Your warmth gives life to the dead,
    your touch makes sinners righteous.

Lord Jesus, in your mercy, heal us;
    in your love and tenderness, remake us.

In your compassion, bring grace and forgiveness,
    for the beauty of heaven, may your love prepare us.

## Psalm 51:1–11

Have mercy on me, O God, according to your loving-kindness;
    in your great compassion blot out my offenses.

Wash me through and through from my wickedness
    and cleanse me from my sin.

For I know my transgressions,
    and my sin is ever before me.

Against you only have I sinned
    and done what is evil in your sight.

And so you are justified when you speak
    and upright in your judgment.

Indeed, I have been wicked from my birth,
    a sinner from my mother's womb.

For behold, you look for truth deep within me,
    and will make me understand wisdom secretly.

Purge me from my sin, and I shall be pure;
    wash me, and I shall be clean indeed.

Make me hear of joy and gladness,
    that the body you have broken may rejoice.

Hide your face from my sins
     and blot out all my iniquities.

Create in me a clean heart, O God,
     and renew a right spirit within me.

## Doxology

Glory be to the Father, and to the Son, and to the Holy Spirit:
as it was in the beginning, is now, and will be for ever.  Amen.

## Scripture Reading

Now among those who went up to worship at the festival were some Greeks. They came to Philip, who was from Bethsaida in Galilee, and said to him, "Sir, we wish to see Jesus." Philip went and told Andrew; then Andrew and Philip went and told Jesus. Jesus answered them, "The hour has come for the Son of Man to be glorified. Very truly, I tell you, unless a grain of wheat falls into the earth and dies, it remains just a single grain; but if it dies, it bears much fruit. Those who love their life lose it, and those who hate their life in this world will keep it for eternal life. Whoever serves me must follow me, and where I am, there will my servant be also." *(John 12:20–26)*

## Meditation

Strapped to an operating table, with my arms stretched out and bound to crosspieces on either side, I felt as if I was on the cross, naked and vulnerable under the sterile sheets. Some years later, while laboring with another child, I tried to focus my breathing and prayers by visualizing a peaceful risen Christ, or Mary, throned in glory, only to find that all I could see was Jesus on a cross, struggling for every breath. Nor is my experience unusual; many women have found a sense of kinship with the suffering Christ through their own struggles to give birth.

## The Lord's Prayer

Our Father in heaven,
> hallowed be your Name,
> your kingdom come,
> your will be done,
>> on earth as in heaven.

Give us today our daily bread.

Forgive us our sins
> as we forgive those
>> who sin against us.

Save us from the time of trial,
> and deliver us from evil.

For the kingdom, the power,
> and the glory are yours,
> now and for ever.  Amen.

## Prayer

O God, we praise you for the small, diminished things: for the health at the edge of our sicknesses, for the moment's quiet in the hours of storm, for the few that held when the many broke and ran, for an answer of love in a lynch mob of hate, for the honest saint in a city of betrayals. We praise you for the minor key, the oblique kindness, the hidden joy. May Jesus Christ understand us in whose name we pray.  Amen.

## Blessing

May the Mother of God, who looked into the face of the dead Christ and knew she could not give him life again, stand by us in our moments of despair and give us cause for hope.

## *Saturday Noon Prayer*

### Opening Sentence

Mary sang the Magnificat, not for herself alone, but for us all to sing it after her.

### Canticle

My soul proclaims the greatness of God,
my spirit rejoices in God my Savior;
> for you have looked with favor on your lowly servant.

From this day all generations will call me blessed;
> for you, the Almighty, have done great things for me,
> and holy is your Name.

You have mercy on those who fear you
> in every generation.

You have shown the strength of your arm,
> you have scattered the proud in their conceit.

You have cast down the mighty from their thrones,
> and lifted up the lowly.

You have filled the hungry with good things,
and the rich you have sent away empty.

You have come to the help of your servant Israel,
for you have remembered your promise of mercy,

The promise you made to our forebears,
to Abraham, Sarah, and their seed forever.


## Psalm 42:1–10

As the deer longs for the water-brooks,
so longs my soul for you, O God.

My soul is athirst for God, athirst for the living God;
when shall I come to appear before the presence of God?

My tears have been my food day and night,
while all day long they say to me, "Where now is your God?"

I pour out my soul when I think on these things:
how I went with the multitude
and led them into the house of God,

With the voice of praise and thanksgiving,
among those who keep holy-day.

Why are you so full of heaviness, O my soul?
and why are you so disquieted within me?

Put your trust in the Most High;
for I will yet give thanks to the one who is the help
of my countenance, and my God.

My soul is heavy within me;
therefore I will remember you from the land of Jordan,
and from the peak of Mizar among the heights of Hermon.

One deep calls to another in the noise of your cataracts;
    all your rapids and floods have gone over me.

You grant your loving-kindness in the daytime;
    in the night season your song is with me,
        a prayer to the God of my life.

## Doxology

Glory to God, our Creator,
to God's most Holy Word,
and to the Spirit, indwelling;
as it was in the beginning,
is now and will be for ever. Amen.

## Scripture Reading

When Jesus arrived, he found that Lazarus had already been in the tomb four days. Now Bethany was near Jerusalem, some two miles away, and many of the Jews had come to Martha and Mary to console them about their brother. When Martha heard that Jesus was coming, she went and met him, while Mary stayed at home. Martha said to Jesus, "Lord, if you had been here, my brother would not have died. But even now I know that God will give you whatever you ask of him." Jesus said to her, "Your brother will rise again." Martha said to him, "I know that he will rise again in the resurrection on the last day." Jesus said to her, "I am the resurrection and the life. Those who believe in me, even though they die, will live, and everyone who lives and believes in me will never die. Do you believe this?" She said to him, "Yes, Lord, I believe that you are the Messiah, the Son of God, the one coming into the world." *(John 11:17–27)*

## Meditation

Even when all despaired when Christ was dying on the cross, Mary, serene, awaited the hour of the resurrection. Mary is the symbol of the people that suffer oppression and injustice. Theirs is the calm suffering that awaits the resurrection. It is Christian suffering, the suffering of the church, which does not accept the present injustices but awaits without rancor the moment when the risen one will return to give us the redemption we await.

## The Lord's Prayer

Our heavenly Father, hallowed is your name.
Your Kingdom is come. Your will is done,
> As in heaven so also on earth.
Give us the bread for our daily need.
And leave us serene,
> just as we also allowed others serenity.
And do not pass us through trial,
> except separate us from the evil one.
For yours is the Kingdom,
> the Power and the Glory
to the end of the universe, of all the universes. Amen!

**Prayer**

Holy One, give us grace to trust in your plan of salvation. Help us to see your work in the world about us; to know that things which were cast down are being raised up, and things which had grown old are being made new, and all things are being brought to their perfection by him through whom all things were made, our Savior Jesus Christ. Amen.

**Blessing**

Let nothing disturb you,
Nothing affright you;
All things are passing,
God never changes.
Patient endurance
Attains to all things:
Who God possesses
In nothing is wanting:
Alone God suffices.

## Saturday Evening Prayer

### Opening Sentence

O come, O come thou haunting sound
that wakes the silenced underground,
that gives the dungeoned words hard won
to claim their place beneath the sun.

### Canticle

I will sing a new song to my God:
    for you are great and glorious,
        wonderful in power and unsurpassable.

May your whole creation serve you
    for you spoke and all things came to be.

You sent forth your Spirit and they were formed:
    for no one can resist your voice.

Mountains and seas are stirred to their depths:
    at your presence rocks shall melt like wax.

But to those who fear you:
    you continue to show mercy.

No sacrifice, however fragrant, can please you;
    but whoever fears God
        shall stand in your sight forever. *(Judith 16:13–16)*

## Psalm 39:5–15

Let me know my end and the number of my days,
    so that I may know how short my life is.

You have given me a mere handful of days,
        and my lifetime is as nothing in your sight;
    truly, even those who stand erect are but a puff of wind.

We walk about like a shadow, and in vain we are in turmoil;
    we heap up riches and cannot tell who will gather them.

And now, what is my hope?
    O God, my hope is in you.

Deliver me from all my transgressions
    and do not make me the taunt of the fool.

I fell silent and did not open my mouth,
    for surely it was you that did it.

Take your affliction from me;
    I am worn down by the blows of your hand.

With rebukes for sin you punish us;
        like a moth you eat away all that is dear to us;
    truly, everyone is but a puff of wind.

Hear my prayer, O God, and give ear to my cry;
    hold not your peace at my tears.

For I am but a sojourner with you,
    a wayfarer, as all my forebears were.

Turn your gaze from me, that I may be glad again,
    before I go my way and am no more.

## Doxology

Glory to God, Source of all being,
Eternal Word, and Holy Spirit;
as it was in the beginning, is now
and will be for ever. Amen.

## Scripture Reading

Christ did not enter a sanctuary made by human hands, a mere copy of the true one, but he entered into heaven itself, now to appear in the presence of God on our behalf. Nor was it to offer himself again and again, as the high priest enters the Holy Place year after year with blood that is not his own; for then he would have had to suffer again and again since the foundation of the world. But as it is, he has appeared once for all at the end of the age to remove sin by the sacrifice of himself. . . .

So Christ, having been offered once to bear the sins of many, will appear a second time, not to deal with sin, but to save those who are eagerly waiting for him. (Hebrews 9:24–26, 28)

## Meditation

> Your work is done,
> You can leave your Cross,
> You can come down to rest, you have surely earned it.

Slowly you slip down, like a man weary of labor
> and drowsy with sleep.
Your mother takes you in her arms.
You rest in peace.

Over your face, calm and serene, there passes a ray of joy.
All is accomplished.
You have made your mother suffer, but she is proud of you.
"Sleep now, my little one, your Mother is watching you."

## The Lord's Prayer

Eternal Spirit,
Pain-bearer, Love-maker, Life-giver,
Source of all that is and that shall be,
Father and Mother of us all,
Loving God, in whom is heaven:
The hallowing of your name echo through the universe!
The way of your justice be followed by the peoples of the world!

Your heavenly will be done by all created beings!
Your commonwealth of peace and freedom sustain our hope and
come on earth.

With the bread we need for today, feed us.
In the hurts we absorb from one another, forgive us.
In times of temptation and test, strengthen us.
From trials too great to endure, spare us.
From the grip of all that is evil, free us.
For you reign in the glory of the power that is love, now
and for ever. Amen.

**Prayer**

Holy Mary, Mother of God, pray for me, a poor sinner. Grant that through the merits of your Son, I may never fall asleep without receiving the forgiveness of the Father, that each night, resting in peace in your arms, I may learn how to die. Amen.

**Blessing**

Christ the Sun of Righteousness shine upon you,
scatter the darkness from your path,
and make you ready to meet him when he comes in glory. Amen.

## *Saturday Night Prayer*

**Opening Sentence**

This is God's manuscript and the Mother who holds it
Is teaching my soul the secrets its phrases bear.

## Canticle

Holy Mary, Mother of God,
> pray for us and for all who are in need.

Holy Mary, Mother of God,
> pray for the hungry and the homeless.

Holy Mary, Mother of God,
> pray for the sick and the frightened.

Holy Mary, Mother of God,
> pray for the wounded and the war-torn.

Holy Mary, Mother of God,
> pray for the sorrowful and the grieving.

Holy Mary, Mother of God,
> pray for the lonely and the despairing.

Holy Mary, Mother of God,
> pray for the tempted and the lost.

Holy Mary, Mother of God,
> pray for the poor and the vulnerable.

Holy Mary, Mother of God,
> pray for the imprisoned and those in danger.

Holy Mary, Mother of God,
> pray for the angry and the scornful.

Holy Mary, Mother of God,
> pray for the persecutors and the violent.

Holy Mary, Mother of God,
> pray for the who suffer and all who sin.

Holy Mary, Mother of God,
> pray for us, now and at the hour of our death.

## Psalm 18:6–20

I called upon the Holy One in my distress
    and cried out to my God for help.

You heard my voice from your heavenly dwelling;
    my cry of anguish came to your ears.

The earth reeled and rocked;
    the roots of the mountains shook;
        they reeled because of your anger.

Smoke rose from your nostrils
        and a consuming fire out of your mouth;
    hot burning coals blazed forth from you.

You parted the heavens and came down
    with a storm cloud under your feet.

You mounted on cherubim and flew;
    you swooped on the wings of the wind.

You wrapped darkness about you;
    and made dark waters and thick clouds your pavilion.

From the brightness of your presence, through the clouds,
    burst hailstones and coals of fire.

The Most High thundered out of heaven;
    you uttered your voice.

You loosed your arrows and scattered them;
    you hurled thunderbolts and routed them.

The beds of the seas were uncovered,
    and the foundations of the world laid bare,
  at your battle cry, O God,
    at the blast of the breath of your nostrils.

You reached down from on high and grasped me,
    and drew me out of great waters.

You delivered me from my strong enemies
    and from those who hated me;
  for they were too mighty for me.

They confronted me in the day of my disaster;
    but you were my support.

You brought me out into an open place;
    you rescued me because you delighted in me.


**Doxology**

Glory be to God,
who made us;
who bears our pain;
and who loves us;
as it was in the beginning,
is now, and will be for ever. Amen.

## Scripture Reading

"Can a mother forget the infant at her breast,
    walk away from the baby she bore?
But even if mothers forget,
    I'd never forget you—never.
Look, I've written your names on the backs of my hands.
    The walls you're rebuilding are never out of my sight.
Your builders are faster than your wreckers.
    The demolition crews are gone for good.
Look up, look around, look well!
    See them all gathering, coming to you?
As sure as I'm the living God" —GOD's Decree—
    "you're going to put them on like so much jewelry,
    you're going to use them to dress up like a bride."
                        *(Isaiah 49:15–18)*


## Meditation

I say that we are wound
With mercy round and round
As if with air: the same
Is Mary, more by name.
She, wild web, wondrous robe,
Mantles the guilty globe,
Since God has let dispense
Her prayers his providence:
Nay, more than almoner,
The sweet alms' self is her
And men are meant to share
Her life as life does air.

## The Lord's Prayer

Our Father, who art in heaven,
    hallowed be thy Name,
    thy kingdom come,
    thy will be done,
        on earth as it is in heaven.

Give us this day our daily bread.

And forgive us our trespasses,
    as we forgive those
        who trespass against us.

And lead us not into temptation,
    but deliver us from evil.

For thine is the kingdom,
and the power, and the glory,
    for ever and ever. Amen.

## Prayer

Be present, Holy One, with us this night. Help us to trust that
you work in the darkness, binding our wounds, healing our hearts.
Help us to trust that, as new life springs from the earth, so new
life emerges from the dark and broken places of the human spirit.
Give us the abiding faith of the Blessed Mother, that we may plant
hope in our sorrow and that of others, trusting that you are ever
working to bring new life from death, through him who died and
rose for us, our Savior Jesus Christ. Amen.

## Blessing

Be the great God between your shoulders
to protect you in your going and your coming;
be the Son of Mary near your heart;
and be the perfect Spirit upon you pouring.  Amen.

# SOURCES

## *Sunday Morning Prayer*

Opening Sentence: "Raegina Caeli," *A Book of Prayers* © 1982 ICEL. All rights reserved. Used with permission.

Canticle: Sisters of the Society of St. Francis, *Community of St. Francis Office Book* (San Francisco, 1996), 35. Used with permission. Hereafter cited as CSFOB.

Psalm: Unless otherwise noted, all psalms are from CSFOB and are used by permission.

Doxology: CSFOB, 18. Used with permission.

Scripture: *Tyndale's New Testament,* ed. David Daniell (New Haven: Yale University Press, 1989). Used with permission.

Meditation: Caryl Houselander, *The Reed of God* (Notre Dame, Ind. Ave Maria, 2006), 80.

The Lord's Prayer: *The Book of Common Prayer* (New York: Church Hymnal, 1979), 97.

Prayer: Penelope Duckworth.

Blessing: Janet Morley, *All Desires Known* (Wilton, CT: Morehouse-Barlow, 1988), 48.

## Sunday Noon Prayer

Opening Sentence: Latin Introit of the Mass of Easter.

Canticle: Magnificat by Katherine M. Lehman. Used with permission.

Doxology: Penelope Duckworth.

Meditation: Amma Syncletica, in Laura Swan, *The Forgotten Desert Mothers* (New York: Paulist, 2001), 20. Used with permission.

The Lord's Prayer: Penelope Duckworth.

Prayer: *A New Zealand Prayer Book* (Auckland: Collins, 1989), 647.

Blessing: Wild Goose Worship Resource Group, Iona Community, Scotland, *A Wee Worship Book* (Chicago: GIA Publications, 1999), 35. Used with permission of GIA Publications, Inc. www.giamusic.com.


## Sunday Evening Prayer

Opening Sentence: "Ave Regina Caelorum," The Marian Library/ International Marian Research Institute http://campus.udayton.edu/mary Used with permission.

Canticle: "Alleluia-verse for the Virgin," from *St Hildegard of Bingen: Symphonia,* ed. Barbara Newman (Ithaca, N.Y.: Cornell University Press, 1988), 125. Used with permission.

Doxology: CSFOB, 12. Used with permission.

Meditation: *The Hymnal 1982* (New York: Church Hymnal, 1985), 190.

The Lord's Prayer: Eugene H. Peterson, *The Message* (Colorado Springs: NavPress, 2005), 1428. Used with permission of NavPress Publishing Group.

Prayer: *The New Zealand Prayer Book*, 108.

Blessing: Penelope Duckworth.

## *Sunday Night Prayer*

Opening Sentence: Reprinted from *Hymns for Morning and Evening Prayer* by Aelred-Seton Shanley © 1999 Archdiocese of Chicago: Liturgy Training Publications, 73. 1800 933-1800 www.ltp.org All rights reserved. Used with permission.

Canticle: John Bell, *Seven Songs of Mary,* Wild Goose Resource Group, Iona, Scotland (Chicago; GIA Publications, 1998), 32-33. Used with permission of GIA Publications. www.giamusic.com.

Doxology: *The Book of Common Prayer,* 46.

Meditation: Rainer Maria Rilke, "Consolation of Mary with the Resurrected Christ," *The Life of the Virgin Mary,* trans. C. F. MacIntyre (Berkeley: University of California Press, 1947), 33. Used with permission.

Prayer: Penelope Duckworth.

The Lord's Prayer: *The Book of Common Prayer,* 97.

Blessing: "Sub tuum praesidium" (4th c.), *A Book of Prayers*. Used with permission.

## Monday Morning Prayer

Canticle: "The Song of Hannah," *A New Zealand Prayer Book,* 82.

Doxology: CSFOB, 18. Used with permission.

Meditation: Penelope Duckworth, "Annunciation: Gabriel speaks."

The Lord's Prayer: Jim Cotter, "Prayer at Night," 1983. Used with permission.

Prayer: Penelope Duckworth.

Blessing: *The Promise of His Glory: Services and Prayers for the Season from All Saints to Candlemas* (London: Church House, 1991), 183.


## Monday Noon Prayer

Opening sentence: *Meister Eckhart: A Modern Translation*, trans. Raymond Bernard Blakney (New York: Harper Torchbooks, 1941), 151.

Doxology: Penelope Duckworth.

Scripture: *Tyndale's New Testament.* Used with permission.

Meditation: Jessica Powers, "The Visitation Journey," *The Selected Poetry of Jessica Powers* (Washington: ICS Publications, 1999), 67. Copyright by Carmelite Monastery, Pewaukee, WI. Used with permission.

The Lord's Prayer: *The Book of Common Prayer,* 97.

The Angelus: Traditional.

Prayer: *The Book of Common Prayer,* 240.

Blessing: *Supplemental Liturgical Texts: Prayer Book Studies 30* (New York: Church Hymnal, 1987), 41.

## Monday Evening Prayer

Opening Sentences: "Of the Word of God," *The Poems of St. John of the Cross,* trans. Kathleen Jones (Westminster, MD: Christian Classics, 1993), 123. Used by permission of Continuum International Publishing Group.

Canticle: Magnificat, *Supplemental Liturgical Texts,* 22–23.

Doxology: *The Book of Common Prayer,* 46.

Meditation: Loretta Ross-Gotta, *Letters from the Holy Ground* (Franklin, Wis.: Sheed & Ward, 2000). Used with permission.

Prayer: Arnold Kenseth, *Sabbaths, Sacraments, and Seasons* (Amherst, Mass.: Windhover Press, 1982), 51. Used with permission.

Blessing: Raissa Maritain, quoted in *Spiritual Writings on Mary,* ed. Mary Ford-Grabowsky (Woodstock, VT: Skylight Paths Publishing, 2005), 186. Used by permission of Skylight Paths Publishing. www.skylightpaths.com.

## Monday Night Prayer

Opening Sentence: M.D. Ridge, "I sing a maid," *Gather Comprehensive* (Chicago: GIA Publications, 1994), 781. Used with permission.

Canticle: *The New Zealand Prayer Book,* 178.

Doxology: CSFOB, 12. Used with permission.

Meditation: Tony Stoneburner, "Annunciation," *Gatherings and Aftermaths* (Golden Valley, Minn.: Limekiln Press, 2006), 1. Used with permission.

The Lord's Prayer: Aramaic version. trans. Vic Alexander, www.v-a.com/bible/prayer.html. Used with permission.

Prayer: Janet Morley, *All Desires Known* (Wilton, Conn.: Morehouse-Barlow, 1988), 10.

Blessing: Rumi, quoted in "The Sama' in the Ghazaliyyat of Moulana Jalaleddin Rumi" by Haideh Ghomi in *Proceedings from the Second European Conference of Iranian Studies* (Rome: Instituto Italiano Per II Medio Ed Estremo Oriente, 1995), 202. Used with permission.


## *Tuesday Morning Prayer*

Opening Sentence: *The Hymnal 1982,* 475.

Canticle: *The New Zealand Prayer Book,* 67–68.

Doxology: *The Book of Common Prayer* BCP, 46.

Meditation: Dorothee Soelle, *On Earth as in Heaven* (Louisville, Ky.: Westminister John Knox, 1993), 76. Used with permission.

The Lord's Prayer: Penelope Duckworth.

Prayer: *All Desires Known,* 10.

Blessing: *Iona Abbey Worship Book,* 87. Used with permission.


## *Tuesday Noon Prayer*

Canticle: Frederica Matthewes-Green, *The Lost Gospel of Mary: The Mother of Jesus in Three Ancient Texts* (Brewster, Mass.: Paraclete, 2007), 111. Copyright 2007 Frederica Matthewes-Green. Available from Paraclete Press; www.paracletepress.com. Used with permission.

Doxology: CSFOB, 12. Used with permission.

Meditation: "Joseph speaks," Alan Jones. Used with permission.

The Lord's Prayer: Cotter, "Prayer at Night." Used with permission.

Prayer: Penelope Duckworth.

Blessing: *Wee Worship Book,* 33. Used with permission.


## *Tuesday Evening Prayer*

Canticle: The Song of Simeon, *The Book of Common Prayer,* 66.

Doxology: CSFOB, 18. Used with permission.

Scripture: *Tyndale's New Testament.* Used with permission.

Meditation: "The Song of Anna," Penelope Duckworth, *Mary: The Imagination of Her Heart* (Cambridge, Mass.: Cowley, 2004), 27–28.

The Lord's Prayer: *The Book of Common Prayer,* 97.

Prayer: *Sabbaths, Sacraments, and Seasons,* 79. Used with permission.

Blessing: Penelope Duckworth.


## *Tuesday Night Prayer*

Opening Sentence: Clare of Assisi in *Francis and Clare: The Complete Works,* trans. Regis J. Armstrong and Ignatius C. Brady (New York: Paulist, 1982). Reprinted by permission of Paulist Press. www.paulistpress.com

Canticle: Magnificat, *The Hymnal 1982,* 437.

Doxology: Penelope Duckworth.

Meditation: George Herbert, "The Flower," in *Seventeenth-Century English Poetry* ed. Miriam K. Starkman (New York: Alfred A. Knopf, 1967), 154.

The Lord's Prayer: *The Book of Common Prayer,* 97.

Prayer and Blessing: Penelope Duckworth.


## *Wednesday Morning Prayer*

Opening Sentence: John of Damascus, quoted in *The Lost Gospel of Mary,* frontispiece. Used with permission.

Canticle: Julian of Norwich in CSFOB, 59. Used with permission.

Doxology: CSFOB, 12. Used with permission.

Meditation: Donald Coggan, *The Servant-Son: Jesus Then and Now* (London: Triangle/SPCK, 1995), 3-4. Used with permission.

The Lord's Prayer: *The Book of Common Prayer,* 97.

Prayer: Penelope Duckworth.

Blessing: Peter de Rosa, *Blessed Among Women* (Dublin: Columba, 2005), 40. Used with permission.


## *Wednesday Noon Prayer*

Opening Sentence: *The Lost Gospel of Mary,* 157. Used with permission.

Canticle: Hildegard of Bingen, "Antiphon for the Virgin," *St Hildegard of Bingen: Symphonia,* 117. Used with permission.

Meditation: Robert Llewelyn, *Memories and Reflections* (London: Darton Longman & Todd, 1998), 138–139.

The Lord's Prayer: Trans. Vic Alexander. Used with permission.

Prayer: Penelope Duckworth.

Blessing: St. Clare of Assisi. From www.StClaresPleasanton.org
Used with permission.

## *Wednesday Evening Prayer*

Opening Sentence: *The Hymnal 1982,* 278.

Canticle: "Magnificat" from *Family Prayers,* by Nick Aiken and
Rowan Williams (New York: Paulist, 2002). Text copyright © 2002
by Nick Aiken and Rowen Williams; edition copyright © SPCK.
Used with permission of Paulist Press.

Doxology: CSFOB, 18. Used with permission.

Meditation: de Rosa, *Blessed Among Women*, 15. Used with
permission.

The Lord's Prayer: Jim Cotter, "Prayer at Night." Used with
permission.

Prayer: *All Desires Known,* 11.

Blessing: Penelope Duckworth.

## *Wednesday Night Prayer*

Opening Sentence: Hajja Muhibba, "The Way of Mary," quoted
in *Blessed Among Women,* 177. Used with permission.

Canticle: Penelope Duckworth.

Doxology: *The Book of Common Prayer,* 46.

Meditation: "Cana," Penelope Duckworth, *Mary: The Imagination of Her Heart*, 101.

The Lord's Prayer: *The Book of Common Prayer,* 97.

Prayer: Penelope Duckworth.

Blessing: *Iona Abbey Worship Book,* 188. Used with permission.


## *Thursday Morning Prayer*

Opening Sentence: Poor Clares of Llongwe, Malawi, from Thomas A. Kane, "The Dancing Church of Africa" (video) (Mahwah, N.J.: Paulist, 1992). Used by permission.

Canticle: Magnificat, translated by Rosemarie Anderson. Used with permission.

Doxology: CSFOB, 18. Used with permission.

Meditation: Martin Luther, *Works,* ed. Jaroslav Pelikan (St. Louis, Mo.: Concordia, 1956), 21:322–323.

The Lord's Prayer: *The Book of Common Prayer,* 97.

Prayer: Penelope Duckworth.

Blessing: *The Promise of His Glory,* 135.


## *Thursday Noon Prayer*

Opening Sentence: Dante. *Paradiso*, The Divine Comedy.

Canticle: Hildegard of Bingen, quoted in *Iona Abbey Worship Book,* 136. Used with permission.

Doxology: *The Book of Common Prayer,* 46.

Meditation: George Bull, "The Low and Mean Conditions of the Blessed Virgin Mary" in *Works* (Oxford, 1846), 110-111.

The Lord's Prayer: *The Book of Common Prayer,* 97.

Prayer: *Iona Abbey Worship Book,* 156. Used with permission.

Blessing: *The New Zealand Prayer Book,* 186.


## Thursday Evening Prayer

Canticle: Francis of Assisi from *Francis and Clare: Complete Works.* Used by permission.

Doxology: CSFOB, 12. Used with permission.

Meditation: Penelope Duckworth, "Hair" from "The Anointing of Jesus: a woman of the city, who was a sinner, speaks," *The Christian Century,* Vol. 114, No. 19, (June 18–25, 1997): 582.

The Lord's Prayer: Peterson, *The Message,* 1428. Used with permission.

Prayer: *The Glenstal Book of Prayer* (Collegeville, Minn.: Liturgical Press, 2001), 66. Used with permission.

Blessing: Penelope Duckworth.


## Thursday Night Prayer

Opening Sentence: *The Hymnal 1982,* 268.

Canticle: "O Mary Don't You Weep," traditional spiritual.

Doxology: Penelope Duckworth.

Meditation: Julian of Norwich, *Showings,* eds. Edmund Colledge and James Walsh (New York: Paulist, 1978), 292, 297–298. Used with permission. Reprinted by permission of Paulist Press. www.paulistpress.com

The Lord's Prayer, Prayer, and Blessing: Penelope Duckworth.

## *Friday Morning Prayer*

Opening Sentence: Julian of Norwich, *Showings,* 342. Used with permission.

Doxology: *The Book of Common Prayer,* 46.

Meditation: Frederick Buechner, *Godric* (San Francisco: Harper & Row, 1980), 96.

The Lord's Prayer: *The Book of Common Prayer,* 97.

Prayer: Arnold Kenseth and Richard P. Unsworth, *Prayers for Worship Leaders* (Philadelphia: Fortress Press, 1978), 28. Used with permission.

Blessing: *Glenstal Book of Prayer,* 66. Used with permission.

## *Friday Noon Prayer*

Opening Sentence: "Mary's Keen," from *Caoineadh na Maighdine* by Gabriel Rosenstock and Roibeard O'Hurdail, (Dublin: Gael-Linn, 1998). Used with permission.

Meditation: Mother Mary and Kallistos Ware, *The Lenten Triodion* (London: Faber & Faber, 1978), 594. Copyright © Monastery of the Protecting Veil, Bussy, France, and Kallistos Ware. Used with permission.

The Lord's Prayer: *The Book of Common Prayer,* 97.

The Angelus: Traditional.

Prayer: *The Book of Common Prayer,* 240.

Blessing: Penelope Duckworth.


## *Friday Evening Prayer*

Opening Sentence: Gerard Manley Hopkins, "The Blessed Virgin Compared to the Air We Breathe," *Poems and Prose,* ed. W. H. Gardner (Harmondsworth, England: Penguin, 1953), 57.

Doxology: CSFOB, 12. Used with permission.

Meditation: Penelope Duckworth, "Shadowing."

The Lord's Prayer and Prayer: Penelope Duckworth.

Blessing: *The Book of Common Prayer,* 133.


## *Friday Night Prayer*

Opening Sentence: Jim Cotter, *Expectant: Verses for Advent* (Harlech, Wales: Cairns Publications, 2002), 4. Used with permission.

Canticle: Magnificat by Penelope Duckworth.

Doxology: CSFOB, 18. Used with permission.

Meditation: Dorothy Day, "Room for Christ," *The Catholic Worker* (December 1945), 2.

The Lord's Prayer: Jim Cotter, "Prayer at Night". Used with permission.

Prayer: *Glenstal Book of Prayer,* 70. Used with permission.

Blessing: *The Roman Missal* © 1973 International Committee on English in the Liturgy (ICEL). All rights reserved. Used with permission.

## *Saturday Morning Prayer*

Opening Sentence: Joseph Raya and Jose de Vinck, *Byzantine Daily Worship,* (Allendale, N.J.: Alleluia Press, 1969), 883. Used with permission.

Canticle: Anselm of Canterbury, quoted in CSFOB, 369. Used with permission.

Doxology: *The Book of Common Prayer,* 46.

Meditation: Margaret Hammer, *Giving Birth: Reclaiming Biblical Metaphor for Pastoral Practice* (Louisville, Ky: Westminster John Knox, 1994), 210.

The Lord's Prayer: *The Book of Common Prayer,* 97.

Prayer: *Sabbaths, Sacraments, and Seasons,* 37. Used with permission.

Blessing: Penelope Duckworth.

## *Saturday Noon Prayer*

Opening Sentence: Luther, *Works,* 21:306.

Canticle: Magnificat in CSFOB, 340–341. Used with permission.

Doxology: CSFOB, 12. Used with permission.

Meditation: Oscar Romero, *The Church is All of You,* ed. and trans. James R. Brockman, (Minneapolis: Winston Press, 1984), 10. Used with permission of the Chicago Province of the Society of Jesus.

The Lord's Prayer: Trans. Vic Alexander Anderson. Used with permission.

Blessing: Teresa of Avila, quoted in *The Glenstal Book of Prayer*, 112. Used with permission.

## *Saturday Evening Prayer*

Opening Sentence*:* Jim Cotter, *Expectant,* 15. Used with permission.

Canticle: CSFOB, 182–183. Used with permission.

Doxology: CSFOB, 18. Used with permission.

Meditation: Michel Quoist, *Prayers,* trans. Agnes M. Forsyth and Anne Marie de Commaille (New York: Sheed & Ward, 1963), 176–177. Gill & Macmillan, Ireland, world rights. Used with permission.

The Lord's Prayer: Jim Cotter, "Prayer at Night." Used with permission.

Prayer: Quoist, *Prayers,* 177. Used with permission.

Blessing: *The Promise of His Glory,* 135.

## Saturday Night Prayer

Opening Sentence: Jessica Powers, from "Pieta," *The Place of Splendor* (New York: Cosmopolitan Science and Art Service, 1946), 78. Copyright by Carmelite Monastery, Pewaukee, Wisc. Used with permission.

Canticle and Doxology: Penelope Duckworth.

Scripture Reading: Peterson, *The Message,* 992–993. Used with permission.

Meditation: Hopkins, "The Blessed Virgin," *Poems and Prose,* 55.

The Lord's Prayer: *The Book of Common Prayer,* 97.

Prayer: Penelope Duckworth.

Blessing: *Iona Abbey Worship Book,* 148. Used with permission.